Cultures of Arab Schooling

Cultures of
Arab Schooling

CRITICAL ETHNOGRAPHIES FROM EGYPT

Edited by
Linda Herrera
Carlos Alberto Torres

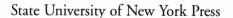

State University of New York Press

Published by
State University of New York Press, Albany

© 2006 State University of New York

For information, address State University of New York Press,
194 Washington Avenue, Suite 305, Albany, NY 12210-2384

Production by Judith Block
Marketing by Anne M. Valentine

Library of Congress Cataloging-in-Publication Data

Cultures of Arab schooling : critical ethnographies from Egypt / edited by Linda Herrera,
Carlos Alberto Torres.
     p. cm.
  Includes bibliographical references and index.
  ISBN-13: 978-0-7914-6901-9 (hardcover : alk. paper)
  ISBN-10: 0-7914-6901-8 (hardcover : alk. paper)
  ISBN-13: 978-0-7914-6902-6 (pbk. : alk. paper)
  ISBN-10: 0-7914-6902-6 (pbk. : alk. paper)
  1. Education—Egypt. 2. Education—Arab countries. 3. Education sociology—
Egypt. I. Herrera, Linda. II. Torres, Carlos Alberto.

LA1646.C85 2006
370.962—dc22

                                                              2005036228

10 9 8 7 6 5 4 3 2 1

This book is dedicated to the memory of Ahmed Abdalla, our friend and engaged colleague, whose legacy as political activist, intellectual, and community worker with marginalized children and youths continues to serve as a model of how to combine passion and integrity with action.

Contents

Acknowledgments

Much of the research presented in this book resulted from the two year involvement of its authors in the Culture and Education in Egypt Working Group (CEEWG) of the Middle East Awards Program (ME Awards) of the Population Council's (PC) West Asia and North Africa Office, Cairo (2002–2003). The Group, coordinated by Linda Herrera, was funded by a grant from the Canadian International Development Agency (CIDA). Many thanks to Barbara Ibrahim, the Regional Director of the PC at the time, and the entire PC staff.

We would not have been able to carry out this work without the help of a talented group of translators, Nawla Basma Darwish, Moushira al-Geziri, Sanaa Makhlouf, and Nur El-Messiri, who allowed us the possibility to read English texts never before available in Arabic, and for an English audience to read texts from authors who have written primarily in Arabic. They also allowed us to communicate across linguistic divides. Moushira diligently translated the lengthy e-mail communications from Carlos Torres who was able to provide substantial exchanges with the CEEWG from its inception.

The CEEWG, in addition to the authors whose work is represented in this book, included the active involvement of a number of colleagues including Fatin Adly, Kamal Maugith, Salwa Gadou, Shebl Badran, Elham Abdel Hamid, Brother Fayez Saad, Salah Subiah, Maha Abdelrahman, and Ahmed Abdalla. Their input, ideas, and experiences percolate throughout this work.

The editors would like to extend a special note of gratitude to Dr. Hassan al-Bialawi, one of the early proponents of Critical Education Theory in Egypt who also happened to be the Undersecretary to the

Minister of Education during the period of our collaborations. He not only provided valuable intellectual guidance to the group, but facilitated our request to the Ministry of Education to obtain research permits to conduct ethnographic research in Egyptian public-sector schools, without which much of this research would not have been possible.

A CEEWG Arabic book, *Qiyam! Julus! Thaqafat al-Ta'alim fi Misr (Stand Up! Sit Down! Cultures of Education in Egypt)* was produced by the Population Council's Cairo office (Herrera 2003) and is available through special request. Chapters 2–5 of this book are based on chapters that appear in that book. Chapters 1 and 6 were previously published by Linda Herrera, albeit in a different form, and are reprinted here by permission. Thanks to C. Hurst & Co. Ltd., for permission to reprint "Islamization and Education in Egypt: Between Politics, Culture, and the Market" (in *Modernizing Islam: Religion in the Public Sphere in Europe and the Middle East*, John Esposito and François Burgat, Editors, 2003: 167–189) and to Elsevier for permission to reprint "Participating in School Upgrading: Gender, Class, and (in) Action in Egypt" (in *International Journal of Educational Development*, Vol. 23, No. 3, 2002: 187–199).

Linda Herrera, The Hague
Carlos Alberto Torres, Los Angeles

Introduction: Possibilities for Critical Education in the Arab World

LINDA HERRERA

AND

CARLOS ALBERTO TORRES

Arab societies have historically placed a high value on knowledge and formal learning. From the rise of Islam in the seventh century to the present, institutions of formal learning, including schools in national education systems of the contemporary period, have been intertwined with major religious, scientific, philosophical, political, economic, and social movements. Despite the centrality of formal education to Arab societies, little is known empirically about learning processes, the cultural, political, and social formation of individuals who pass through the education system, and the everyday life of schools. This book, resorting to critical ethnographic methodologies and description, offers rare glimpses into the life of schools in a contemporary Arab society and proposes a series of hypotheses and empirical analyses about the relationships between schooling and the social order. It does so from a perspective of critical theory practiced by scholars from the region, also a rare avis in an Arab society.

This study views teachers, schools, students, and the State in a relational perspective. But it is neither an evaluative study nor a study primarily of educational politics. It is not a study per se of public policy, or of educational policy, and it is not per se a study of administration and bureaucracy. It is a study that takes seriously the need to use qualitative

1

methodologies to address issues of social production, reproduction, quality, and democratization.[1] This study attempts, among other things, to show not only what schooling potentially looks like when there is attention to quality in the learning process, but, conversely, what happens when there is not.

Certain overlapping themes run throughout this volume such as the pyramidal and antidemocratic nature of schooling as it is often structured and practiced, the impact of social movements—particularly Islamist movements—on school cultures, the ways in which a neoliberal market logic contributes to a demise of the teaching profession and increases social inequity, the growing cultures of resistance to authoritarianism, the gap between official policies and the social and material realities of schooling, and the desire on the part of educators and youths to make schooling a more meaningful, respected, and transformative social endeavor.

Why Study Education through Critical Theory and Critical Ethnography?

> "…there is no way we can escape the social world in order to study it."
> —Hammersley and Atkinson, 17

From the outset we will outline our understanding of both "Critical Ethnography" and "Critical Social Theory," remaining aware of the wisdom of the exiled Menchevique Russian social scientist, Pitirin Sorokin, who once said that sociologists say what everybody knows but in a language few can understand. Therefore, our purpose is not to obscure the discourse by incorporating a new jargon, but simply to make explicit the processes and foundations that oriented our research for more than two years.

Critical Social Theory (CST) has made impressive contributions to our understanding in the social sciences, particularly linking critique and utopia, leaving us a legacy from which the scholars involved in the project of this book work. It is evident that Critical Social Theory, its pedagogical counterpart, Critical Pedagogy (CP), and one of its methodological frameworks, Critical Ethnography (CE), are slowly reaching domains of education in the Arab world, but they have a long way to go. The contributors of this book have come together out of a firm conviction that a critical sociology of Arab education can serve to inform educators, reformers, policy-makers, and diverse publics towards a greater understanding of issues relating to social justice, participation, and democracy, and also their antitheses, injustice, passivity, and authoritarianism.[2]

This book project began in 2002, when a group of educational researchers—all of whom identify broadly with a critical perspective—came together from universities and research centers based in Egypt under the umbrella of the Culture and Education in Egypt Working Group of the Population Council in Cairo.[3] The group met regularly to read and discuss critical education literature with the aim of eventually undertaking critical research on school cultures. It transpired early in our explorations and deliberations that our research should be grounded in the tradition of critical ethnography, an approach that, in the words of education anthropologists Bradley Levinson and Dorothy Holland, is "fundamentally local and ethnographic, yet moves beyond the school to examine links between local cultural practices and the community, the region, the state, and the economy" (1996, 2). Yet it was also clear that most members of the group were versed mainly in quantitative research methods and lacked experience in interpretive qualitative research.[4] We therefore integrated methodological inquiries into our discussions about how to achieve a critical approach to Arab education.

Critical Ethnography is useful as a foundational method of inquiry for a number of reasons. Canadian sociologist and ethnographer Steve Jordan offers a good summary when he argues that CE draws from a large body of diverse yet compatible theoretical traditions including phenomenology, symbolic interactionism, ethnomethodology, neo-Marxism, Feminism, Semiology, and Cultural Studies. Jordan concludes that what distinguishes CE from conventional ethnographic approaches are several themes: first, CE is "focused on how ethnographic research could be connected with the wider political economy of capitalism"; second, CE focuses on power and social inequality; third, CE accepts the premise that the "contemporary world is organized through often exploitative and oppressive social relations, [hence marking] a decisive break with conventional forms of ethnography; fourth, CE "aims to enhance and empower subaltern groups through the research process itself," and finally, since dominant forms of social and political theory are considered implicated in ruling Western capitalist societies, a theme "pursued by critical ethnography is the refinement, or restructuring, of social and political theory" (Jordan 2003, 88–89). This last point brings us closer to the elective affinity (to put it in a Weberian fashion), between Critical Ethnography and Critical Social Theory in our research.

Here, the sobering and insightful voice of Freire helps to chart the journey of addressing social reality for social transformation when he argues:

> Most professors do not address objective reality. Rather, they address analysis of objective reality found in books and articles. They turn this into the object of knowledge, within struggle for power, focusing upon accumulated knowledge. This impedes approximation to reality. The learning exercise is turned into a struggle around representations that we have of reality, and ideological struggle, addressing power that we do know how to manipulate. Consequently, the dialogue that should emerge from such analysis is no longer a mediated dialogue leading to reality. It is an alienating metaphysical 'dialogue' about an abstract 'reality' that has no real meaning (Torres 1994, 23).

As Carlos Alberto Torres argues, identities are social constructions with material and historical bases; indeed, they are based on perceptions of knowledge, experience, and power, particularly, what knowledge is (or should be considered) legitimate and should count, what experience should be celebrated and learned from, and how power can be negotiated among different forms of knowledge and experiences. Yet, as Joan Scott has argued so forcefully, the same notion of experience, which seems to underlie the notion of identity is something historically, culturally, and discursively produced (1992, 12–19). Alas, as Michael Apple has also so aptly argued for more than two decades, the connections between power and knowledge become central to any practical agenda of research and policy making in education, particularly in this new era of the conservative restoration (1982, 1986, 1993). This perception, of the ubiquities of power in any social relationship, forms the foundation of any CE.

Moreover, CE leads not simply to comprehension, but a calling into question of existing cultural traditions that conceal relations of domination to be overcome through the transformation of consciousness.[5] If, in the best of the Freirean education for liberation tradition, the role of education is the transformation of consciousness—, it should not be a surprise that CE could play a powerful role in research aiming at transformative educational models. This, of course, speaks to the universalization of a mode of critique and a model of analysis which is transparent, normative, and analytical and is gaining more hold in academia world-wide. In a context like the Arab world, where education researchers are taking potential risks by embracing CST, it becomes an even more powerful mode of analysis.

That research has consequences never escaped the researchers involved in this study, particularly those making their living in the often difficult conditions surrounding social research in Egypt. Indeed, it is clear that our research was developed in opposition to the mainstream research conducted in Egypt and much of the region (and for that matter, in terms of its dominant orientation, elsewhere in the world).[6] Thinking about the difficulties and potential consequences of this research reminded us of a poignant statement made by Paulo Freire regarding university professors:

> ...There is no creativity without the risk of creating....The matter of freedom is basic for the search, for risk. However, we cannot fall into a naïve idealism when thinking it is possible to create a "province of freedom" outside a specific society where the material conditions of that society work against the affirmation of freedom (1994, 142–144).

Aware of Freire's caution, we now turn to addressing possible reasons for why interpretive, qualitative educational research, which includes ethnographies of school cultures in the Arab states, has been so sparse.[7]

Challenges to Critical Research in Arab States and Beyond

It is likely that critical, empirically based, interpretive modes of inquiry have been underrepresented—albeit by no means absent—in the Arab world due to structural and political constraints that inhibit critical approaches, and also due to a certain culture of scholarship that favors theoretical and quantitative research over applied and qualitative research. To a large degree, and similar to academic cultures in other regions, the culture of scholarship in the Arab world privileges the role of the *mufakir* (thinker), but less so that of the *mubahith* (researcher), a situation that finds some parallels with the *pensador* of Latin America.[8] Notwithstanding some notable exceptions, scholars derive prestige, legitimacy, and cultural capital in their ability to engage with theory at the macro level and in their capacity to conduct scientific (large scale) survey research. Such professional values leave little space for exploring new areas of inquiry informed by empirical research at the micro level, reflexivity, doubt, risk-taking, creativity, and innovation, some of the hallmarks of interpretive ethnographic approaches.

To exacerbate the situation, universities and research centers in the Arab world, the hubs of knowledge production, tend to be located within authoritarian or surveillance systems that seriously impede academic freedom. In numerous countries of the region universities are heavily monitored by state security apparatuses that interfere in any number of university affairs—often in the name of cultural preservation or national security—in areas such as faculty travel, topics for research and conferences, curricular materials, and scholarly exchanges (Herrera 2006). Universities are also especially vulnerable to political instability and military conflict. Civil, regional, and international conflicts in the Middle East region drain material and human resources (hence the high degree of brain drain), impede scientific research and production, and often lead to increased repression at university campuses (Human Rights Watch 2005; Mazawi 2005, 154–156).

The widely circulated and debated Arab Human Development Reports (UNDP 2002, 2003) point to how, in addition to some of the above factors, the quality and quantity of academic production in the region has suffered due to inflexible and sometimes rigidly nationalistic approaches to knowledge. The reports' authors call for more regional and international cooperation, the reform of knowledge institutions towards more flexibility, and the pursuit of more translations of scholarly and literary works into Arabic, because "openness, interaction, assimilation, absorption, revision, criticism and examination cannot but stimulate creative knowledge production in Arab societies" (UNDP 2003, 8). An opening to new ideas and ways of knowing can also lead to what the report's lead author, Nader Fergany, (2005) calls an "Arab renaissance."

As other scholars are apt to point out, the crisis and deterioration of academic freedoms and scholarly production cannot be blamed entirely on government constraints, geopolitics, and relatively closed scholarly communities. There also appears to be a crisis of knowledge production whereby scientific inquiry and intellectual rigor are being replaced by superstition and ideological religosity. As renowned Cairo University professor of political science, Mustapha Kamel El-Sayed, explains: "We must admit that society no longer believes in scientific research. Seventy-five per cent of what Egyptians read is about religion" (quoted in *Al-Ahram Weekly* 2004).

A parallel with the conservative Christian restoration in the United States should not go unnoticed. With their purposeful mixing of religion and politics, one may conclude that the current Bush administration's disregard for actual scientific proof (as demonstrated in efforts to put forward "intelligent design" as a biblically inspired explanation for evolution) may not drastically differ from the reported situation in Egypt.[9] Among the many roles of critical, rational, research in the contemporary period, therefore, is to disentangle ideology from theology, expressions of extremism from religious faith, and to examine the structural factors that may account for the rise of fundamentalist movements.

Struggles for Democratic Change in the Arab World

Despite the many impediments to critical research and action in the Arab world, there are clear signs of invigoration of academic and research communities who continuously struggle for democratic change. Prodemocracy movements have recently emerged on university campuses and snowballed with impressive rapidity. The Ninth of March Committee for the Independence of Universities and the Egyptian Association for Support of Democracy are two such groups. They call for greater freedom in universities (by way of higher salaries and less security interference) and in society (Human Rights Watch 2005, 4). The former also calls for political reforms, including the end of the Emergency Law, and the release of (Islamist) colleagues from jail (*Al-Ahram Weekly* 2005).

In the area of educational research, a more critical oriented research grounded in ethnographic, interpretive, and participatory methodologies in and on the region has been emerging in past years. This literature, much of which is situated in the fields of development and educational reform, spans a range of topics including curriculum development and teacher empowerment in Palestine (Nakleh and Wahbeh 2005), the politics of development aid and in-school technology in Egypt (Warschauer 2004), problems associated with international aid and the importance of grassroots alternative development in Oman (Chatty 1996), schooling and changes in gender norms in Jordan (Adely 2004), and cultures and uses of literacy in Morocco (Wagner 1993).

There also exists a critical mass of education projects in the Arab region grounded in principles of Critical Pedagogy. They include, to mention just a few, the adult literacy programs of CARITAS in Egypt, the schools and myriad community initiatives of the Association of Upper Egypt for Education and Development, and the curriculum, research, and training programs of the Qattan Centre for Educational Research and Development (QCERD) in Palestine. An especially well-documented initiative has been the community school movement in Egypt, a participatory, community-based, child-centered, initiative spear-headed by UNICEF, in 1992, to reach girls in some of the poorest and most remote areas of Upper Egypt (Zaalouk 2004). Among the striking manifestations of community schools have been that despite being under the management structure of the Ministry of Education, teacher/facilitators exhibit far more autonomy in their work than in mainstream schools, and appear to be endeavoring on a "new culture of learning." (166). The movement has influenced aspects of mainstream education through a process of diffusion and provided new paradigms for training, curriculum development, and one-classroom schools.[10] The project takes the view that educational reform should be "a liberating force that unleashes the highest potentials of learners.... It transforms schools into safe spaces where relations are redefined, as opposed to institutions that reinforce existing relations of power and oppression" (163). Considered together, these developments represent the stirrings of change in academic, development, and critical research communities.

Striving for an Education for Liberation

We hope this book can make a modest contribution to the emerging literature, debates, projects, and movements for educational change. At the very least, the publication of research findings can alert the reader to a new awareness, shape the climate in which both political discussions are undertaken and practical decisions made, and may even directly stimulate particular sorts of action. Yet we anticipate that some critics may argue that this book could have been done differently: that the research could have been conceived using the standard frameworks; that researchers could have pursued other logic of proofs in their own case studies; that Critical Ethnography as a method could have been conducted for a longer period, and in more areas of the country.

While theoretically all of this is possible, the practical constraints, and the differential in power in academic institutions (not to mention limited resources), needs to be taken into account when inspecting the results, the language of analysis, and the logic of proof presented in this book. We deem the possibility to impact the world of educational research in Egypt and the larger Arab world through the dissemination of this research as very likely (there is an Arabic version of some of the key papers already in circulation).[11] Less likely is the immediate effect on the systems. The circumstances of the geopolitics of the Middle East, the role of globalization in the intersection between culture and power in the region, and the role of international aid on educational reform, cloud the practical implications for critical educational change. Yet, this book draws attention to two key sets of issues, and could serve as a sourcebook for serious educational reform in the future.

First, the studies contained in this book demonstrate there is a small, yet vibrant and growing, community of researchers in Egypt who do not abide by the rules of the status quo and are able to seek alternative theories, data, and interpretation. The quality and diversity of studies in this book testify to this effect. A second set of issues is the connection between the personal biography and the location of the researchers in the use of theory, methods, and research infrastructure. To ensure a dialogue among the researchers, and to secure funding and permission for this research, took a good deal of negotiating and navigating complex national and international institutional contexts. The fact that the two editors do not hold nationality of an Arab country—though Linda Herrera speaks Arabic and lived and worked in Egypt for seventeen years—demonstrates the possibility of international collaboration as long as people converge on a similar set of values and, more importantly, practices. We converge on similar values that facilitate these studies including the appreciation for Critical Pedagogy and Critical Theory as a theoretical paradigm. We converged on similar sets of methodological strategies—the reliance on Critical Ethnography as a method of inquiry. Finally, we also succeeded due to collegiality, friendship, and commitment, particularly of those located in national organizations who were cognizant that their findings would be unpopular in many circles.

While these are valid and valuable reasons for the production of this book, even more importantly, what these essays have in common and the reason that we have been able to collaborate over a long period of time, is the mutual respect and affection we have shown to each other. This is so, clearly, because we all share Paulo Freire's perspective when he tells us that every book he has written is a report of a particular phase of his pedagogical and political experience. The politicy of education is one of the key concepts that we have shared in trying to understand education within the Egyptian context. The other important lesson from Freire (and one that in our opinion differentiates the radical and critical perspective from the establishment one), is a commitment to social transformation.

Paulo Freire addresses this perspective in his book *Politics and Education:*

> The comprehension of the limits of educational practice absolutely requires political clarity on the part of educators in relation to their project. It demands that the educator assumes the political nature of his/her practice. It is not enough to say that education is a political act just as it is not enough to say that political acts are also educative. It is necessary to truly assume the political nature of education. I cannot consider myself progressive if I understand school space to be something neutral, with limited or no relation to class struggle, in which students are seen only as learners of limited domains of knowledge which I will imbue with magic power. I cannot recognize the limits of the political-educative practice in which I am involved if I don't know, if I am not clear about in whose favor I work. Clarifying the question of in whose favor I practice, puts me in a certain position, which is related to class, in which I devise against whom I practice and, necessarily, for what reasons I practice—that is, the dream, the type of society on whose behalf I would like to intervene, act, and participate (1998, 31).

Education as a possible dream, a dream of liberation, is the lynchpin that articulates the research effort of this book. The utopian dream of liberation, in the best of the Freirean tradition, and the critique of banking education helps portray the landscapes of knowledge as described in the next section.

Landscapes of Knowledge: Lessons Learned in this Work

The contributors to this volume are all concerned with education in the Arab region, yet due to the simple fact of the research group having been located in Egypt, the chapters are all based on ethnographic fieldwork conducted in and on Egypt. Given Egypt's role in the Arab region as a major exporter of educational expertise, teachers, texts, and political and social trends, it is an especially fitting country to profile. Individual authors had full autonomy in selecting their research topics and there was no systematic attempt to include a nationally representative sample of school cultures. Given the diverse interests of individual authors, a rich cross section of Egyptian society, from urban poor and slum communities (chapters 2–3), rural communities (chapter 5), to urban middle-class communities (chapters 1, 4, & 6) are represented.

For those employing the logic and modes of inquiry and engagement of critical ethnography for the first time, the method itself raises new awareness for "researcher" and "researched" alike. Referring to her open-ended interviews with teachers, Iman Farag notes:

> It was apparent that none of them [the teachers] had ever been the subject of this kind of interest before, and if some of the material in this research paper hits the nail on the head, it is due to the novelty of the experience for the researched subjects and the researcher alike" (chapter 4).

For others, the method initially caused some difficulties and awkwardness. As Ahmed Youssof Saad experienced as an Egyptian "insider," he could not initially perceive the research environment in a critical or analytical light (chapter 3). His familiarity with the environment and modes of interactions initially "dulled his observational capabilities." Researchers were sometimes the objects of teacher suspicions and had difficulty justifying their presence in the schools and convincing school communities that they were not agents of the state (chapters 3–5). When conducting her research, Linda Herrera was chided by an intimidating school director who declared: "This is not research you're doing. Who told you this research? What you're doing has no value whatsoever. I advise you to stop wasting your time!" But we are joined in the conviction that Critical Ethnography is far from a waste of time. Rather, it is a necessary step in the arduous processes of social understanding and transformation. Despite expressing some initial and justifiable suspicions, most teachers were eager to participate, share their experiences, express their grievances, offer ideas, and generally have their voices heard and recorded in the hope that they could play a part in movements towards reform.

The authoritarian form of school governance came up in different ways in most all papers. The intersection between state authoritarianism and banking education is self-evident in the Egyptian context. Consider, for instance the arguments advanced by Kamal Naguib who relates: "The elaborate hierarchies in the workplace and in schools are not designed to facilitate the management processes, but to reproduce symbols of authority and relations of control and submission" (chapter 2). Moreover, for those interested in efficiency of, and performance in the systems, the strictures of banking education make matters very difficult and change is straightjacketed by: "The inflexible static curricula, rigid examination practices, heavily bureaucratic school administration, and constant inspections, all [of which] reflect the authoritarianism of school governance" (chapter 2).

Among the daunting findings of these studies is that schools reflect the culture of the oppressed, not the civilization of the oppressed, as Brazilian scholar Jose Eustaquio Romão so eloquently defends in redefining Freire's perspective (Romão 2003). A main argument, well-represented in the work of Ahmed Yousof Saad, is that schools breed the personality of the oppressed, "... bearing all the elements of the culture of oppression, sensing helplessness and insecurity in the face of the violence imposed by the master, policeman and landlord who use force, and by the bureaucrat who can get papers moving or stop them" (chapter 3). The culture of the oppressed is reflected in the ways schools are complicit in the reproduction of the despotic personality. Naguib cogently shows how despotism is reproduced in schools. He argues that:

> The prevalent culture of despotism inside schools, as in the whole society more generally, is founded on the monopoly of the decision-making processes and the negation of difference and alternate points of reference. Relations...are based on dominance and submission. Clearly, the culture of despotism works at reproducing the despotic personality (chapter 2).

Further along these lines political scientist Ahmed Abdalla posits that "The problem in Egypt is not the 'impossibility' of constructing a democratic system, but rather the 'difficulty' of establishing it under the prevalent despotic values inherited from ancestor and forefathers. (n.d., 7).[12]

Paulo Freire's insights on authoritarianism seem to concur with Abdalla's views:

> As one might expect, authoritarianism will at times cause children and students to adopt rebellious positions, defiant of any limit, disci-

pline, or authority. But it will also lead to apathy, excessive obedience, uncritical conformity, lack of resistance against authoritarian
discourse, self-abnegation, and fear of freedom (Freire 1998b, 40).

Instead of experiencing schools as places where they can dream,
express intellectual curiosity, form community, and prepare for the
future, students often experience schools as places that thwart their creativity and suppress their desires. Schools tend to reproduce fear, not
love or respect. Naguib quotes a school director who affirms, "this
[young] age needs fear more than love. There is not sufficient time for
all of that."

A number of authors are especially disturbed by what they see as the
rise of extremism in schools. As Saad elucidates, "A mature reading of the
world has become a less likely possibility for those people who, in addition to poverty, sickness, and ignorance, are haunted by a ghost even
more destructive of human consciousness; religious extremism" (chapter
3). We must be clear that by "religious extremism" the authors refer to an
ideology that distorts religion to breed sectarianism and prejudice against
the "other," and a closing-up of society. We maintain that religion,
whether Islam, Christianity, or any other religion, is not inherently
extremist or progressive, it is what situated actors make it.

In recent decades, an important front of conflict, at least from the government's perspective, has been the unofficial Islamization of schooling in
Egypt. Educational Islamization should be understood partly as a political
movement, but also as a long-standing dilemma in Egyptian education of
how to simultaneously raise children in the proper Islamic way, while educating them in principles of secular nationalism and preparing them for
employment in global markets determined in a moment of late capitalism.
According to the research presented in this book, Egyptian parents are to a
large—and growing extent—pious and conservative, and the moral education of their children is of paramount importance. But the government's
question is how to create the proper conditions for educating children in a
pious, or Eastern/ Islamic model, while at the same time preventing fundamentalism?[13] This dilemma is documented in Linda Herrera's first chapter
on Islamic private schools, wherein she shows how Islamism can manifest
in different ways: it can lead to politicization of school cultures, to more
profit-driven schooling in which Islam becomes a commodity, and to
youth-led movements towards either extremism or greater pluralism of
practice and ideas (chapter 1).

Clearly, religious extremism represents just one aspect of an impoverished school and teacher culture. Apathy can be as detrimental to learning as extremism. Fadia Maugith documents cases of teachers and librarians who never read, who have no curiosity about the world, and who mechanically transmit to their students packed curricula in such a disinterested and unimaginative way that they cannot possibly instill a love of learning and joy of discovery in the young (chapter 5).

As in other countries, privatization of education has led to growing social inequality in Egypt. As Saad points out:

> The slogan 'Education for all' . . . comes to mean equality of opportunity in climbing aboard the ship of education without necessarily implying the ability to stay aboard or to save one's place till the end of the voyage. With the rise of privatization of schooling, formal education has contributed to ever-widening social inequality (chapter 3).

By far the starkest manifestation of unchecked market relations in education are found in the phenomenally widespread practice of private lessons. Private lessons are so prevalent that the sum spent on them by Egyptian families, as Saad reports, "has almost become equivalent to the state budget for education (19 billion Egyptian pounds)." Farag links the phenomenon of private lessons to class struggle, which she sees as taking place in an unfettered education market. She astutely suggests:

> Private lessons . . . may be considered a form of class struggle . . . which, like all struggles, contains non-ethical means and ends. This struggle has been left to the mechanisms of the market and has essentially led to a privatization of part of the education sector in the context of a society driven towards economic liberalism without a minimum level of social rights (chapter 4).

Perhaps Naguib offers the most unsettling critique of private lessons when he suggests that teachers "by pursuing the objective of giving private lessons, a practice that allows them to secure a livelihood, . . . sacrifice their mission as educators" (chapter 2).

The discourse on privatization, profit, and corruption of teachers needs to be placed in the context of the dynamics of globalization and the standard neoliberal recipes for educational reform. The analytical premises and strategies employed by the World Bank and the institutions associated with the Washington Consensus are based on supply-side economics (Torres 2002). The neoliberal agenda includes a drive towards privatization and decentralization of public forms of education, a movement towards educational standards, a strong emphasis on testing, and a focus on accountability. With regard to accreditation and universalization, major efforts are underway throughout the world to reform academic programs through accreditation processes and various strategies that produce increased homogeneity across national boundaries.[14]

At a macro political-economic level, these chapters document some of the ways in which market trends and a growing "neoliberal mentality" have distorted a range of relations that take shape around schooling. Not only do we see the expansion of profit-driven schooling whereby students and parents become customers and teachers, exploitable workers, but the very vocation of teaching, so revered and put upon a pedestal, is in fact becoming increasingly based on business exchanges through private lessons. Farag explains:

> The teaching profession has clearly been negatively affected by...market trends. Moreover, it seems that the 'vocational' dimension of the profession has been 'against the current.' For whether we view teaching with the criteria of competency (professional) or equity (social), it would seem that what is asked and expected of teachers is contrary to the wave of neoliberal tendencies (chapter 4).

The questions raised are by no means easy, for teachers repeatedly expressed that they do not earn enough salary to live a minimum dignified life. Teachers' financial insecurity is exacerbated by the hierarchical and antidemocratic nature of the school machinery in which they are professionally located. The situation does not fare much better for school administrators who must work within rigid hierarchical structures and who lack any significant decision-making capacity. Despite some attempts by the Ministry of Education and NGOs to democratize at least certain aspects of schooling (chapter 6), teachers repeatedly pointed out that they were subject to increasingly anti-democratic regulations. They were also subject to constant recriminations and monitoring by an array of supervisors from the national, district, and local school levels (chapters 2–4). Educational inspectors and a range of follow-up evaluation committees hinder what little autonomous space teachers possess in the classroom. One teacher tells us, as reported by Farag, that "These inspectors are no more than disgusting creatures coming to find mistakes, not to look at reality, they waste time and generate paperwork" (chapter 4).

As a consequence of financial insecurity, lack of autonomy, and impoverished school cultures, it comes across clearly that for the most part neither teachers nor administrators derive much satisfaction, let alone creative pleasure, from their work. Needless to say, this experience may not be idiosyncratic to Egypt but part of a larger universal educational experience.[15] Much of the research reported in the chapters in this book reflect both the culture of submission to bureaucratic authority, and the rebellion, disgust, or occasionally the indifference of students, parents, teachers, and administrators, to that authority. Even the most simple act could reveal the most complex social and psychological aspects involved in the tasks of teaching and learning in the life of the school.

This book offers interesting glimpses about the qualities of a good teacher within the restraints of the system. Whereas the seeming standard bureaucratic understanding of teaching is that of "a pedagogical enterprise that aims at transmitting the maximum amount of information to students" (chapter 2), or as someone who can "impart knowledge and maintain surveillance" (chapter 4), alternate understandings exist. A student expressed that, "A good teacher is kind to us, solves our problems, cares about us, and is humane" (chapter 3). Within such a diverse, struggling, and rich cultural landscape, we can find conscientious, creative, and committed teachers who manage to realize their ideals of what it means to be a teacher (chapers 4–6).

Through their journeys into critical ethnography the authors suggest that the struggle for a liberatory education is still a long haul in Egypt and the Arab region more generally. Iman Farag eloquently explains: "Education ... is a powerful tool of political control, whether as a tool for dreams, or for liberation. To be precise, knowledge liberates while the institution controls: such is the structural problematic" (chapter 4). Yet as this book shows, school environments are places in which contradictions and confrontations may open up spaces for alternative constructions, new pedagogical initiatives, true learning, and eventually a renewed sense of utopia and hope.

Forging Critical Communities

How can we move from interpreting and understanding difficult and sometimes bleak findings in research within an analytical and normative approach that emphasizes utopia and hope? Is cynicism the answer? Is stoicism the answer? Or worse yet, is skepticism the answer leading (as it sometimes does as an illness of our contemporary culture), to nihilism? Let us reject all those portraits of the future, arguing that our conviction, for the need to develop a transformative social justice learning model, may offer a basis for hope. One of us has defined else-where, that transformative social justice learning, as a social, political, and pedagogical practice, will take place when people reach a deeper, richer, more textured and nuanced understanding of themselves and their world (Torres 2003).

Not in vain has Freire always advocated the simultaneous reading of the world and of the word. Based on a key assumption of critical theory—that all social relationships involve a relationship of domina-tion, and that language constitutes identities—transformative social jus-tice learning, from a symbolic perspective, is an attempt to recreate various theoretical contexts for the examination of rituals, myths, icons, totems, symbols, and taboos in education and society. It is an examina-tion of the uneasy dialectic between agency and structure, setting for-ward a process of transformation. From a sociological perspective, transformative social justice learning entails an examination of systems, organizational processes, institutional dynamics, rules, mores, and regu-lations, including prevailing traditions and customs, that is to say, key structures which, by definition, reflect human interest. We hope that the essays contained in this book help the process of transformative social justice learning in Egypt and beyond, and that if there is at times a somber picture, we should not overlook the richness of the educational experience and the struggles taking place in those settings; there are also the immense qualities of imagination and cultural actions for freedom. They never let us, even when marginal or in a subordinate position, perish in the abyss of nihilism, stoicism, or skepticism.

Notes for Introduction

1. Quality is often measured by various quantifiable inputs such as expenditure on schooling, class size, equipment, teacher education, and out-puts based on exam scores. This dominant approach suffers from a serious con-ceptual problem in that it leaves out the learning process. As Joel Samoff and Bidema Carrol so cogently argue in reference to the World Bank, an institu-tion that has been dominant in setting the terms of the debate in education policy circles, "inattention to the learning process becomes itself an obstacle to improving quality. Seeking broadly applicable patterns, commonly termed

'best practices,' is a further obstacle, since to be effective education must be con-tinually modified to suit unique and local circumstances. . . . [T]he learning process remains a lower priority concern for the World Bank" (Samoff and Carrol 2003, 30).

2. For literature in Arabic on the need for a critical sociology of education in the Arab world see Hassan Al-Bialawi (1993).

3. The contributors to this volume were all members of the Culture and Education in Egypt Working (CEEWG) group of the Middle East Awards Program of the Population Council (MEAwards), West Asia and North Africa Office which was coordinated by Linda Herrera and funded by a grant from the Canadian International Development Agency (CIDA). The CEEWG members consisted of Kamal Naguib, Ahmed Youssof Saad, Iman Farag, Fadia Maugith, Fatin Adly, Kamal Maugith, Salwa Gadou, Shebl Badran, Elham Abdel Hamid and Linda Herrera. Carlos Alberto Torres served as an advisor to the group from the earliest stage and traveled to Egypt in December 2003 on the occasion of the formal dissemination of the group's Arabic findings. Among the other participants in various meetings of the group were the late Fayez Saad of the Jesuit Cultural Centre in Alexandria, Hassan al-Bialawi of the Ministry of Education, Salah Subiah of the adult education unit at CARITAS, the late Ahmed Abdallah, political scientist and director of The al-Jeel Center, and Maha Abdelrahman, sociologist at the American University in Cairo.

4. In their review of a sample of master's theses from education faculties in Palestinian universities, Khalil Nakhleh and Nader Wahbeh of the Al-Qattan Center for Educational Research and Development (QCERD) in Ramallah, took issue with the prevalence of quantitative research. They found the overwhelming majority of studies not only quantitative is design, but detached from any signifi-cant education reform efforts, and "uninformative, rarely insightful, redundant, and uninquisitive" (Nakhleh and Wahbeh 2005, 14).

5. The recently deceased French philosopher and member of the French Socialist party, Paul Ricoeur, so aptly called this transformation of conscious-ness the "hermeneutic of suspicion" (1986).

6. For a discussion of the notions of legitimation in capitalism, see the classic text of Jürgen Habermas, *Legitimation Crisis* (1975). For a discussion of compensatory legitimation in educational policy, see Raymond Allen Morrow and Carlos Alberto Torres, *Social Theory and Education. A Critique of Theories of Social and Cultural Reproduction* (1995).

7. Two examples of school ethnographies from the Arab region in English are Linda Herrera's, *Scenes of Schooling: Inside a Girls' School in Cairo* (1992), and Orit Ichilov and André Elias Mazawi's, *Between Church and State:*

Life-Hisotry of a French Catholic School in Jaffa (1996). A number of excellent anthropological studies have been published on aspects of educational culture and social change in the Arab region such as Dale F. Eickelman's *Knowledge and Power in Morocco* (1985), Hamed Ammar's *Growing Up in an Egyptian Village* (1954), and Gregory Starrett's *Putting Islam to Work* (1998) to name just a few. These works, while they deal with aspects of formal schooling, cannot be characterized particularly as school ethnographies.

8. The concept of *mufakir* in the Arab world resembles that of the *pensador* in the Latin American tradition, a notion that goes back to the ninetieth century and linked to debates and struggles to organize the new postcolonial societies and nations. As Carlos Alberto Torres has argued in a previous work, the *pensador* emerged in Latin America as a synthesizer of new models of social consciousness and eventually of a new common sense. They were partisan to the degree that they charted new territories trying to create new intellectual spaces, hence they could not claim neutrality of any kind, and they adopted an engaged reflexivity that took many of them to exile because "Governments fear the effect of their hortatory presence on the internal political process and the influence of their voice upon students and professor partisanships" (Torres 1994, 16).

9. Just to document this fact, the recent report in several U.S. newspapers of an ongoing campaign by conservative groups to train Congress staffers—many of whom work in Congress because they themselves wish to pursue a career of politics in the future—through workshops at lunch in which the word of God, as prescribed in the Bible, is interpreted as a commanding call of higher order to answer pressing political issues. There is no question that this project puts the notion of democratic representation at serious risk.

10. The concept of "diffusion" relates to how change penetrates from the locale of a particular setting to other aspects of society. As Zaalouk posits, "change is an organic, not a mechanical, process. It does not occur sequentially or as the result of an act of legislation. Nor does change occur at an equal pace in all parts of a system.... Normally once a movement has developed into a critical mass it will work its way to other parts of the system" (2004, 148).

11. Different versions of chapters 2, 3, 4, and 5 of this book were published in the Arabic volume, *Qiyam! Julus! Thaqafat al-Ta'alim fi Misr* [Stand Up! Sit Down! Cultures of Education in Egypt, edited by Linda Herrera (2003)]. This volume is available by request to the Population Council's West Asia and North Africa office based in Cairo, Egypt.

12. The editors would like to offer a word of caution in the use of the concept despotism. Unlike the notion of "Oriental despotism" which has taken on an ahistoric and essentializing understanding, despotism as described in these

works, relates to real social and political-economic contexts—contexts that are mutable—and not to some innate civilizational trait. The words of political scientist and anthropologist Mahmood Mamdani forcefully cautions against "civilizational" discourse. He posits: "There is reason to be hugely skeptical of claims that describe civilizations discretely and identify civilization histories with particular geographies and polities. One has to distinguish between civilization and power" (2004, 32–33).

13. Religious extremist, or "fundamentalist" movements have been defined as being "infused with the spirit of religious bigotry and political authoritarianism" (Postman, 1994 147)—a definition, incidentally, that refers to Christian fundamentalism in the United States.

14. Two elements radically condition the formulation of public policy: privatization and the reduction of public spending. These two policies are highly compatible, and in fact, privatization can be considered an important strategy for achieving reductions in public spending. The privatization policies require additional explanation. These policies are crucial elements of the reforms oriented towards promoting markets and as such, they are an important policy tool of neoliberalism. On the one hand, the pressure of fiscal spending is reduced by the privatization of public sector enterprises. On the other, privatization is also a powerful instrument for depoliticizing the regulatory practices of the state in the area of public policy formation. That is, privatization plays a pivotal role in the neoconservative and neoliberal models because "purchase of service contracting is both an administrative mechanism for addressing the particular issues of the social legitimacy of the state involved in direct social services and an attempt to borrow from the managerial ethos of private enterprise and (entrepreneurial development), systems of cost-benefit analysis and management by objectives" (Culpitt 1992, 94).

Neoliberals and neoconservatives have argued that the state and the market are two social systems that are diametrically opposed and that both are considered as real options for providing specific services (Moran and Wright 1991). Why then does there appear to be a preference for the market over the state? Neoliberals and neoconservatives consider that markets are more versatile and efficient than the bureaucratic structures of the state for numerous reasons. Markets respond more rapidly to technological changes and social demand than the state. Markets are seen as more efficient and cost-effective than the public sector in the provision of services. Finally, market competition will produce more accountability for social investments than bureaucratic policies.

15. See, for example, research findings in six countries by Carlos Alberto Torres, Seewha Cho, Jerry Kachur, Aurora Loyo, Marcela Mollis, Akio Nagao and Julie Thompson, "Political Capital, Teachers' Unions and the State. Value

Conflicts and Collaborative Strategies in Educational Reform in the United States, Canada, Japan, Korea, Mexico, and Argentina." Los Angeles, UCLA, manuscript. This study has been supported by a grant from the Pacific Basin Research Center-Soka University, a grant from the Pacific Rim Center of the University of California, and a grant from the Spencer Foundation. Research currently being undertaken in fourteen countries, investigating the impacts of globalization on teachers' and students' lives and curriculum, offers some glimpses of dissatisfaction with school cultures that resemble our findings in Egypt (Carlos Alberto Torres with the collaboration of Liliana Olmos and Roberth Rhoads). Globalization and Educational Reform: K-12 and Higher Education Reform in Argentina, Brazil, Mexico, United States, Canada, Egypt, South Africa, Korea, Taiwan, Japan, China, Portugal, Italy and Spain. Paper prepared for a conference at UCLA, August 4–9, 2003, mimeographed.

References

Abdalla, Ahmed. n.d. *Democratization in Egypt.* Institute for Developing Economies, Japan External Trade Organization, Visiting Research Monographs.

Al-Ahram Weekly. 2004. To keep thought alive (by Fatemah Farag). March, Issue no. 681, 11–17.

Al-Ahram Weekly. 2005. University staff joins protests (by Gihan Shanine). 26 May–1 June, Issue no. 744.

Al-Bialawi, Hassan. 1993. *Fi'Ilm Ijtima` al-Madrasa* [Of a Sociolology of the School]. Cairo: Al-Markaz al-Qawmi lil-bahuth al-tarbawiyya wa al-ta`limiyya. [in Arabic].

Ammar, Hamed. 1954. *Growing Up in an Egyptian Village: Silwa, Province of Aswan.* London: Routledge & Kegan Paul.

Apple, Michael W. 1982. *Education and Power.* Boston and London: Routledge.

———. 1986. *Teachers and Texts; A Political Economy of Class and Gender Relations in Education.* New York and London: Routledge.

———. 1993. *Official Knowledge. Democratic Education in a Conservative Age.* New York and London: Routledge.

Culpitt, Ian. 1992. *Welfare and Citizenship. Beyond the Crisis of the Welfare State?* London, Newbury Park and New Delhi: Sage.

Eickelman, Dale F. 1985. *Knowledge and Power in Morocco: The Education of a Twentieth-Century Notable*. Princeton, NJ: Princeton University Press.

Fergany, Nader. 2005. Freedom, Justice, and Good Governance in Arab Countries. *ISIM Review*, no. 16: 32–33.

Freire, Paulo. 1994. in *Paulo Freire on Higher Education. A Dialogue at the National University of Mexico*. In Miguel Escobar, Alfredo L. Fernández, and Gilberto Guevara-Niebla with Paulo Freire. Albany: State University of New York Press.

———. 1998b. *Teachers as Cultural Workers*. Boulder, CO: Westview Press.

———. 1998. *Politics and Education*. Los Angeles: UCLA Latin American Center Publications.

Habermas. Jürgen. 1975. *Legitimation Crisis*. Trans. by Thomas McCarthy. Boston: Beacon.

Hammersley and Atkinson. 1995. *Ethnography: Principles in Practice*. London: Routledge.

Herrera, Linda. 1992. Scenes of Schooling: Inside a Girls' School in Cairo. *Cairo Papers in Social Science* 15 (Monograph 1).

———. 2003. *Qiyam! Julus! Thaqafat al-Ta'alim fi Misr* [(Stand Up! Sit Down! Cultures of Education in Egypt)]. New York and Cairo: Population Council [(in Arabic)].

———. 2006. Higher Education in the Arab World. In *International Handbook of Higher Education*, ed. James J. F. Forest and Philip Altbach, 409–421. Springer.

Human Rights Watch. 2005. Reading between the "Red Lines": The Repression of Academic Freedom in Egyptian Universities. Vol. 17, no. 6.

Ichilov, Orit, and André Mazawi. 1996. *Between Church and State: Life-History of a French-Catholic School in Jaffa*. Frankfurt am Main: Peter Lang.

Jordan, Steve. 2003. Critical Ethnograpy and the Sociology of Education. In *The International Handbook on the Sociology of Education. An International Assessment of New Research and Theory,* ed. Carlos Alberto Torres and Ari Antikainen. Lanham and Boulder: Rowman and Littlefields.

Levinson, Bradley, and Dorothy Holland. 1996. The Cultural Production of the Educated Person: An Introduction. In *The Cultural Production of the*

Educated Person: Critical Ethnographies of Schooling and Local Practice, ed. Bradley Levinson, Douglas Foley, and Dorothy Holland, 1–54. New York: State University of New York Press.

Mamdani, Mahmood. 2004. *Good Muslim, Bad Muslim: America, the Cold War, and the Roots of Terror*. New York: Pantheon Books.

Mazawi, André Elias. 2005. Contrasting Perspectives on Higher Education Governance in the Arab States. In *Higher Education: Handbook of Theory and Research,* ed. J.C. Smart, Vol. XX, 133-189. London: Springer.

Monsivais, Carlos. 1997. *Los rituales del caos*. Mexico: ERA.

Moran, Michael, and Maurice Wright. 1991. *The Market and the State: Studies in Interdependence*. New York: St. Martin's Press.

Morrow, Raymond Allen, and David D. Brown. 1994. *Critical Theory and Methodology*. Thousand Oaks, London and New Delhi: Sage .

Morrow, Raymond Allen and Carlos Alberto Torres. 1995. *Social Theory and Education. A Critique of Theories of Social and Cultural Reproduction*. New York: State University of New York Press.

Nakhlen Khalil, and Nader Wahbeh. 2005. Doing Research on Improving the Quality of Basic Education in Palestine. Paper submitted to the "Global Conference on Education Research in Developing Countries," sponsored by Global Development Network. Held in Prague, Czech Republic, 31 March–2 April.

Postman, Neil. 1994. *The Disappearance of Childhood*. New York: Vintage Books.

Ricoeur, Paul. 1986. *Lectures on Ideology and Utopia*. Ed. George H. Taylor. New York: Columbia University Press.

Romão, Jose Eustáquio. Forthcoming. Pedagogia Sociológica ou Sociologia Pedagógica. Paulo Freire e a Sociologia da Educação. In *Educação Crítica and Utopia. Perspectivas Emergentes Para o Século XXI*, ed. António Teodoro and Carlos Alberto Torres. Porto: Afruntamento.

Samoff, Joel, and Bidemi Carrol. 2003. From Manpower Planning to the Knowledge Era: World Bank Policies on Higher Education in Africa. *Prepared for the UNESCO Forum on Higher Education, Research and Knowledge*, 15 July.

Scott, Joan W. 1992. Multiculturalism and the politics of identity. *October* 61, (Summer): 12–19.

Starrett, Gregory. 1998. *Putting Islam to Work: Education, Politics, and Religious Transformation in Egypt*. Berkeley: University of California Press.

Torres, Carlos Alberto. 1994. Introduction. In *Paulo Freire on Higher Educaiton: A Dialogue at the National University of Mexico*, ed. Miguel Escobar, Alfredo L. Fernández, and Gilberto Buevara-Niebla with Paulo Friere. Albany: State University of New York Press.

———. 1999. Critical Theory and Political Sociology of Education: Arguments. In *Critical Theory in Educational Discourse*, ed. T. J. Popekwitz and L. Fendler. New York: Routledge.

———. 2002. Expert Knowledge, External Assistance and Educational Reform in the Age of Neoliberalism: A Focus on the World Bank and the Question of Moral Responsibilities in Third World Educational Reform. Paper prepared for the meeting "Extending the Boundaries of Democracy: Two Decades of Education Reform and Inclusion Policies." December 9th—December 13th 2002, Bellagio, Italy.

———. 2003. Paulo Freire, Education and Transformative Social Justice Learning. Paper prepared for the Fifth International Conference on Transformative Learning. Teachers College, Columbia University. New York, October 20–22.

United Nations Development Program (UNDP). 2002. *Arab Human Development Report 2002: Creating Opportunities for Future Generations*. New York: United Nations Publications.

United Nations Development Program (UNDP). 2003. *Arab Human Development Report 2003: Building a Knowledge Society*. New York: United Nations Publications.

Wagner, Daniel A. 1993. *Literacy, Culture, and Development: Becoming Literate in Morocco*. Cambridge: Cambridge University Press.

Wahbeh, Nader Atallah. 2003. Teaching and learning science in Palestine: Dealing with the New Palestinian Science Curriculum. *Mediterranean Journal of Educational Studies* 8 (1): 135–159.

Warschauer, Mark. 2004. The rhetoric and reality of aid: Promoting educational technology in Egypt. *Globalization, Societies, and Education (2)*3, 377–390.

Zaalouk, Malak. (2004) *The Pedagogy of Empowerment: Community Schools as a Social Movement in Egypt*. Cairo and New York: American University in Cairo Press.

1

Islamization and Education: Between Politics, Profit, and Pluralism

LINDA HERRERA

Summary

In Egypt as in much of the Middle East, a convergence of factors including the rise of Islamist movements, the liberalization of the economy (which has resulted in increased privatization of schooling), and the influence of youth cultures are contributing to changes in the educational terrain in unforeseen ways with little understood consequences. Through a review of education debates and ethnographic inquiries into private sector Islamic schools, this chapter highlights how, despite a centralized and heavily monitored formal education sector, nonstate parties including Islamists, businesspersons, and female youths, are influencing the practices and processes of schooling. While members of Islamist movements often reinforce and exacerbate authoritarian and politicized education cultures, and members of the business sector sometimes trivialize Islam to the profit motive, groups of female urban youths may contribute to an opening of school cultures towards a questioning of norms which can lead to greater plurality of practices and ideas.

Introduction: Schooling and Overlapping Interests

Schools serve as socializing institutions of children and youth par excellence. Notions about citizenship, the competencies needed to function in bureaucratized societies, meanings about what it means to be a member of communities based on national, religious, class, craft, gender, regional, and global affiliations—to name only a few—are transmitted in innumerable ways through formal schooling. Yet transmission reflects only a fraction of what occurs in the complex environment of schooling. School cultures reflect overlapping interests and influences. Even in centralized and heavily state-monitored formal education sectors, such as in Egypt, the process and outcome of schooling is vastly differentiated. Far from functioning as a static social institution under the domination of a hegemonic state, the school represents a potentially dynamic site of political and cultural struggle and social transformation.

Through a review of education debates and ethnographic inquiries into private sector Islamic schools, and by examining the role of different school actors, from government bureaucrats, school owners, teachers, to youths themselves, this chapter reviews how manifestations of the Islamization of education have been tremendously varied, from reinforcing authoritarian education cultures and trivializing and reducing Islam to the profit motive, to contributing to a greater plurality of practices and ideas. Among the challenges of critical research is to identify the spaces and conditions under which practices grounded in critical reflection lead to greater plurality of practices and ideas.

State Education: Centralized, Secularized, and Islamized

In Egypt, as in much of the Arab region, schools operate within the parameters of a centralized and heavily bureaucratized management structure. All Egyptian children from age six are legally obliged to attend eight years of basic education that consists of the primary (grades 1–5) and preparatory (grades 6–8) stages. Egyptians can choose from two parallel systems of education: the more secular and widespread general education schools under the administration of the Ministry of Education (MOE), which make up roughly 80 percent of all schools, or the more Islamically oriented al-Azhar or Azharite schools under the administration of the al-Azhar Institutes Department of al-Azhar University that are open only to Muslim students. Azharite schools follow the same curriculum as general schools, with the addition of an intensive program in religious studies in Quranic recitation (*talawa*), Quranic exegesis (*tafsir*), and Islamic jurisprudence (*fiqh*). The two systems generally track their students to different paths of higher education via their secondary schools: Azharite schools to al-Azhar University, one of the oldest Islamic universities (est. 972 AD), and general schools to national state universities. Under certain conditions, graduates of Azharite secondary schools can join national universities and vice versa. In both systems, the curriculum is both standardized and centralized. Currently Azharite institutes are often perceived (particularly among urban middle classes), as schools of last resort because of government policies that require them to admit students who have failed in general schools. Nevertheless, Azharite schools continue to enjoy prestige within certain rural and urban communities where formal religious training is regarded as a form of cultural and social capital.

Our concern here is with general secular schools that have served, with the rise of the modern state, as sites of national citizen building for all Egyptians regardless of religion. The designation of secular may seem a misnomer because general schools are by no means devoid of religious instruction. From first grade on, all students are required to take a mandatory religion class, either Islam or Christianity, depending on the student's religion. Perhaps more significant, the secular nature of schooling may be further called into question when we consider that in Egypt, as in many other Arab and Muslim majority states, the upbringing aspect of schooling is expressed in more explicit terms than in other parts of the world. As Gregory Starrett notes, "Muslim states have followed a different course to modernity, insisting explicitly that progress requires a centrally administered emphasis upon moral as well as economic development" (Starrett 1998, 10). Implicit in the upbringing component of schooling is the attempt—by planners and educators—to transmit to students, regardless of their religious affiliation, a sense of belonging to a Muslim society with a culture and history embedded in Islam. Islamic messages and symbols are formally incorporated into the daily life of schools through, among other means, rituals, religious passages in textbooks, religious signs and posters displayed throughout schools, and the emphasis, by teachers, on an "Islamic disposition."

Apart from state-designed forms of promoting identification with Islam, schools, like the rest of society, have been undergoing a marked process of Islamization. A combination of social, political, and economic factors account for the gradual Islamization, of both society and formal education, since the 1970s. The rise of Islamist, pietistic, or resurgence movements (especially since the 1967 Arab defeat in the war with Israel), the substantial influx of money and a new form of piety by returned workers from the Arab Gulf countries, changes in communications technology, popular culture, and consumer culture have all influenced the ways in which Islam has been publicly staged, debated, and interpreted (Eickelman and Anderson 1999; Salvatore 1999). Furthermore, the relative opening of civil society, the subsequent spread of organizations—including Islamic organizations—under the umbrella of civil Islam (Abdelrahman 2005; Sullivan 1994, Kandil 1998; Norton 1995), and the increased privatization of schooling at all levels, has been part of a broader, neoliberal economic agenda (Kienle 2001).

Contests for Control over National Education

Sensing a loss of control over its education sector, and fearing a radicalization of its institutions, factions of the Egyptian government undertook a highly public and systematic crackdown on schools and universities to curb the processes and manifestations of Islamization. The Ministry of Interior has been monitoring schools for signs of Islamist political tendencies since the early 1980s, but it was not until 1991 that a new minister of education put the issue of ideological control of schools in the public spotlight. In the view of the Minister of Education, Dr. Husayn Kamal Baha Eddin (1991–2004), schools and universities were slipping dangerously out of the state's control and into the hands of Islamist extremists, thereby posing a threat to the country's national security.

Baha Eddin, a pediatrician and former secretary general of the Nasser-era ideological watchdog group, the Youth Organization (*Munazamat as-Shabab*), became minister in 1991 by presidential appointment and under politically volatile circumstances. His predecessor, Fathi Sorour, was abruptly transferred to the position of speaker of the People's Assembly replacing Rifaat al-Mahjoub who was slain in Cairo by members of a militant Islamic group. During that period, Egypt experienced a civil war (of sorts) between state security forces and militant Islamist groups, many of whom were based in Upper Egypt, the southern region of the country. The involvement of high school and-university-age students in militant organizations, and growing reports that schools were being used as recruiting grounds for militant groups, prompted the Minister to characterize schools as "hatcheries of terrorism" (*tafrikh al-irhab*) (Baha Eddin 1997, 55).

Baha Eddin introduced the concept of education as a cardinal component of national security, on par with the military, and by so doing abandoned decades-old socialist-era rhetoric of education being a service of the state, like health care or infrastructure development. In a book written by the minister in 1997, *Education and the Future* (*Al-Ta'alim wa al-Mustaqbal*), he explains:

> The first aspect of a new educational policy is that education is an issue of national security. . . . The use of the term 'national security' [referred] for a long time to military power, the shield that protects the nation from all dangers that threaten it. This term changed in the period after World War I and before the end of the Cold War because specialists, politicians, and high-ranking military officers realized that national security [refers to] more than mere military power (84).[1]

To assess the extent to which schools were actually threatening national security, the Chancellor to the Minister of Education, Dr. Abd al-Fattah Galal, prepared a report for the education committee of the People's Assembly (the Egyptian parliament) in May 1993.[2] He discovered that ninety schools and three hundred teachers (listed by name) had links to illegal Islamist political groups including *al- Jama'a al-Islamiyya* (*Jama'a*), the largest Islamic militant group in Egypt; *al- Jihad,* the militant Islamist group believed to have masterminded the assassination of President Anwar Sadat; and *Ikhwan al-Muslimeen* (The Muslim Brotherhood), the reformist—and by that time nonviolent—Islamist group that was founded in 1928. Most of the schools with supposed links to militant groups were concentrated in Upper Egypt, specifically the southern cities of Qena and Asyout. In an interview, Baha Eddin asserted that his own investigations revealed that extremism was not limited to specific geographic regions but was a nationwide phenomenon (*Middle East Times* 1995).

A weekly semiofficial magazine conducted its own investigation into religious extremism in schools and reported that the Muslim Brotherhood was buying up preschools and elementary schools, and that *Jihad* exerted control over teacher training institutes. It provided the example of a secondary school in Asyout that was used as a recruiting ground and hideout for the *Jama'a*. Teachers purportedly preached to students about the apostate Egyptian government, played recorded sermons of the dissident Shaykh Omar Abdul Rahman, distributed the illegal *Jama'a* magazine, *Murabitun*, to students, and discriminated against Christian students by expelling them from classes and forbidding them from running in class elections. At a religious institute also located in Asyout, an English teacher and spokesman for the *Jama'a*, instructed his students to write English from right to left because Arabic, the sacred language of the Quran, is written right to left (Roz al-Youssef 1993, 27). The report cited other cases of how school teachers in Upper Egypt lured students to their organizations through extracurricular activities such as soccer camps, book fairs, cultural events, and free private tutoring sessions at mosques. Another report revealed that militant Islamic groups were using schools in a small village in Upper Egypt to store illegal arms (Maughith 1998). Stories also abounded about how teachers were either forcing or scaring young girls into wearing an Islamic uniform.

Baha Eddin, with the mobilization of state security forces, set out to regain control of the nation's schools and universities and further hinder the growth of militant political activism among the youth. He pursued a strategy that included intensifying the screening and surveillance of students in teacher education colleges, and purging Islamist teachers, administrators, and materials from schools.

Screening and Surveying University Students

Universities have long been the sites of political activism. Leftist student politics dominated Egyptian university campuses from the 1960s to the mid-1970s, when Islamists took them over. In part this was due to the tacit support of the regime of Anwar Sadat, who used them to counter the growing influence of the leftist student movement. By 1977, Islamists student politics were a force to be reckoned with (Abdalla 1985, 226). Islamist student leaders dominated student councils and student associations provided copious social services for students such as free tutoring, used books, subsidized housing, meals, and used clothing.

The minister brought to the fore how Islamists had strategically infiltrated colleges of education, hubs of Egypt's future teachers, in an attempt to eventually capture the nation's youth. In a 1993 interview, Baha Eddin warned of the gravity of the situation:

[E]xtremists have penetrated the education system and are trying to gain control of it, thereby gaining control of twelve and a half million students who will be the pillar of our nation in ten years from now.... The extremists found that the best way to accomplish their goals was to concentrate in the Colleges of Education.... [If we don't do something about it] hundreds of teachers will graduate as believers in their ideas and this will be a catastrophe! (*Akhbar al-Hawadith* 1993)

The education colleges were the first targets of Baha Eddin's national security campaign on university campuses. The Higher Council for Universities set up committees in 1992 to implement new selection criteria that included security checks to ensure that incoming students did not belong to any "misleading groups" that might "demolish the educational process" (Baha Eddin 1997, 56). In a meeting with professors from a college of education in 1993, Baha Eddin stressed that it was the job of the faculty to abolish terrorism and thereby serve as the eyes for state security forces (*Al-Ahram* 1993). For the first time, and despite chronic shortages of teachers, a situation arose where qualified applicants were being refused entry into colleges of education, and graduates were being denied teaching posts due to security reasons.

When a separate Ministry of Higher Education (MHE) was formed in 1997, its new minister, Moufid Shehab, former president of Cairo University, expanded security and surveillance measures on campuses. He required all students living in student hostels to submit detailed information about their families and themselves to university authorities. Students living off campus were required to supply their college with a landlord's letter confirming where and with whom they resided. The MHE also undertook proactive strategies and developed programs to provide a range of services and summer camps for students similar to those already provided by Islamist student organizations.[3] As the MHE carried out measures to thwart Islamist influence in universities, the Ministry of Education (MOE) sought ways to cleanse its primary, preparatory, and secondary schools of Islamist penetration.

Purgings of Teachers and Materials

The education sector underwent a series of censorship sweeps and purges. For the most part the targets were religious and political materials, and educators who attempted to influence children towards greater religiosity through tactics of coercion or fear.[4] District education supervisors scoured school libraries for any unauthorized, and potentially politically subversive materials such as religious books, political pamphlets, and cassette tapes or videos of religious sermons. In response to critics from among the secular liberal and religious camps who argued that book censoring contradicted Baha Eddin's stated policy of liberal democracy, he responded:

> We [censor] books that support extremist ideas that are against the valid teachings of Islam. Psychologically speaking, a child is a person who does not have a formed character.... He cannot fight ... so it is the State's responsibility to take care of the child and not leave him to face unhealthy situations.... I don't approve of censorship, but I have the duty to protect the child physically, psychologically, and mentally. Until he is formed he has to be under the protection of the family and the State. (Baha Eddin in *Akhbar al-Hawadith* 1993)

Purging materials from schools proved a somewhat easier task than purging public-sector schoolteachers and administrators who, as tenured government employees, are protected by socialist-era labor laws. Instead of outright dismissals, educators were transferred—or banished—to other government positions sometimes hundreds of kilometers away where they would not have contact with children.

Between the summer of 1993 and March of 1995, roughly one thousand educators were transferred out of schools and into other government posts. Baha Eddin stated, in an interview in 1995, that he was prepared to eliminate ten thousand teachers if necessary (Al-Hayat 1995, 17). As late as 2004, Baha Eddin fired thousands of extremist secondary school teachers (Human Rights Watch 2005, 71 citing *Cairo Times* 2004). Some teachers were penalized because they tried to persuade or compel female students to wear an Islamic uniform of some sort. Others used nonapproved religious materials in the classroom, such as the especially widespread cassette-recorded sermons of the *Torture of the Graves* (*Azab al-Qabr*). Children were often forced to listen to these sermons which describe in terrifying detail how hideous snakes, agonizing beatings, and a fiery underworld awaited them in the afterlife if they failed to strictly abide by the tenets of Islam.

Many teachers and school administrators penalized during this period claimed to have been unfairly singled out and punished without good cause. Unable to rely for their defense on the Teachers' Syndicate, a historically ineffectual institution devoid of any real power, growing numbers of educators turned to litigation, and many of them won their cases against the MOE. A number of the litigants were linked to Islamic schools, public and private sector general schools with a self-proclaimed Islamic character. By the early 1990s, Islamic schools, particularly the private Islamic schools (*madaris Islamiyya al-khassa*), became the targets of governmental crackdowns.

Islamic Schools: Maintaining the Form, Altering the Content

Private Islamic schools refer to general schools that attempt, within the strict confines of a fixed form, to alter the cultural and ideological content of the everyday life of the school. They are not attached to Azharite institutes, do not belong to a unified association of Islamic schools, and do not necessarily depend on the *ulama* (the Muslim scholarly class), for religious supervision. Rather, individual school directors and staff, many of whom have not had any formal religious training, determine their school's policies regarding religious content and practices. Private Islamic schools first began appearing in Egypt in the 1970s, contemporaneous with other new types of Islamic institutions such as clinics, hospitals, banks, and nursery schools. These schools cater to a range of urban social classes, from the urban poor to the urban elite. Their fees range from a modest LE 250 per year (approx. $41), to a much heftier LE 12,000 per year (approx. $2000). By conservative estimates, private Islamic schools numbered roughly two hundred twenty in 2003, however this number does not include the scores of public-sector schools that have adapted a self-proclaimed Islamic identity. Like most private schools, private Islamic schools are overwhelmingly an urban and northern phenomenon and are concentrated in Greater Cairo and Alexandria.[5]

Private Islamic schools are under the administrative authority of the MOE, and, like all other private schools, are obliged to operate according to nationally set guidelines with regard to curriculum, exams, and all major aspects of school organization. As private schools, they have some leeway in hiring staff, and have an independent owner and board of directors. To ensure that schools abide by correct official procedures and practices, district, regional, and national supervisors regularly inspect them, sometimes several times a day. Even with this degree of heavy surveillance, these schools attempt to provide an alternative educational experience.

One such private Islamic school, Fatima School for Believers (a pseudonym), was established in 1985. Located in a densely populated, poor industrial area of Cairo, the school offered the promise of a more Islamic environment and higher educational standards than the neighboring overcrowded and rundown government schools. Its tuition fees were relatively modest, LE 345 per year for elementary school, and LE 425 per year for preparatory school. The school was owned and run by Mr. Abdallah, (also a pseudonym), a graduate of al-Azhar University's education section. He earned the financial capital to build the school facility after a four-year employment stint in Saudi Arabia, where he worked as a high school history teacher.

A member of the Muslim Brotherhood, Abdallah regards schools as the most effective institutions for *dawa* (the call), to proper Islam, a position in keeping with the teachings of the Brotherhood's main ideologue, the late Hassan Al-Bannah. According to this formulation, schools contain a missionary dimension and serve as vehicles for proselytizing. Yet proselytizing does not refer to attempts to convert non-Muslims to Islam, but to convert Muslims from the wrong path of Islam to the straight or correct path. Abdallah argues that, in order to grow and fulfill their obligations as correct Muslims, children should be raised in a religious environment that adheres to Islamic law, as opposed to what he called the secular and corrupt environment of government schools. His school is coeducational because a single-sex school would not have been financially viable even though, by his own admission, single-sex education is preferable in Islam. He attempts to keep students separated by sex; at the primarily level, boys and girls share a classroom but sit on opposite sides of the room; at the preparatory level, classrooms are single-sex.

As a general private school under the authority of the MOE, Fatima School strictly follows the government curriculum. Since end-of year exams are nationally administered and based on the standardized national curriculum, teachers tend not to alter the official curriculum to any great degree, despite the stated temptation of some to do so. The overall mode of school governance, as in socially equivalent private and public schools, could be described as pyramidal and authoritarian (see Naguib, chapter 2; and Saad, chapter 3); the school management structure is principally hierarchical; classroom interactions are based on principles of submission and obedience to adult authority, and corporal punishment is rife. The school, then, does not attempt to change the norms of mainstream school management, but provides an alternative schooling experience by cultivating in its school community a more Islamic—as opposed to Egyptian or secular—identity.

For example, adult school authorities at Fatima school try to socialize students into using Islamic, as opposed to pagan (*jahiliyya*) greetings and exaltations. Teachers continuously emphasize that on entering or leaving a room, or on greeting someone, students should never say *ahlan* (hello), *sabah al kheir* (good morning), or *ma'a salama* (good-bye), but should only use the correct religious salutation, *as-salamu aleykom* (peace be upon you). The use of Islamic language extends to other classroom contexts. In most Egyptian schools, it is commonplace for classmates to applaud a colleague's achievement at their teacher's prompting. Applause is forbidden at Fatima school since it had no apparent precedent in Islam; the correct way of rewarding a child is to invoke the name of God, because He alone is responsible for all achievement. At the teacher's prompting, a class would praise a colleague by saying in unison: *allahu akbar wa allahu hamid* (God is great and we praise him). The student receiving the recognition would respond, *lil-lah nishkur* (to God we give thanks). Teachers punish any child who carelessly blurts out a profane greeting or response in lieu of the correct Islamic one, usually by way of whacking the student's palms or upper arm with a stick.

Another important site for the cultivation of an alternative identity is the *tabour*, or morning assembly, a mandatory nationwide ritual in all Egyptian schools. The *tabour* signifies the start of the school day and represents a time when the entire school community congregates and communicates. In most schools, the morning assembly follows a fairly standardized and militarized routine: children line up by class group in the courtyard, perform exercises in unison, stand at attention while teachers and students make announcements about school events, read out some of the headlines from a national semiofficial newspaper, and recite a short selection from the Quran or hadith. The peak of the assembly is when the entire study body faces the Egyptian flag situated at the center front of the courtyard, and sings the Egyptian national anthem, *Biladi, Biladi* (My Homeland, My Homeland) with the accompaniment of an accordion or portable keyboard (Herrera 1992, 10–12).

Similar to many schools around the country with Islamist tendencies, Fatima School for Believers subverts the flag saluting and national
anthem singing on the grounds they are pagan—akin to idol worship-
ping—and signify support of the illegitimate Egyptian government. Yet
at Fatima School these nationalistic rituals are not eliminated outright,
but modified and infused with an Islamic content that carries an overtly
subversive political meaning.

The assembly begins with a drum roll because it is widely believed
that while musical instruments are not permitted in Islam, the drum is.
The students perform light exercises in the military drill-like fashion of
other schools, however, instead of keeping time by shouting one, two,
three, four, in rhythmic unison, they proclaim: the glory of God! thanks
be to God! there's no God but God! God is Great! They repeat this
sequence four times. They then continue with the other elements of the
assembly—announcements, news, prayer—until the drum roll sounded
again, indicating the time for the singing of the national anthem. The
students, however, do not sing the Egyptian national anthem, "*Biladi,
Biladi,*" but an alternative anthem entitled, "*Illahi, Illahi*" (My God, My
God), a track sung at Muslim Brotherhood meetings in Egypt and whose
familiar melody, is identical to that of *Biladi, Biladi* (composed by pop-
ulist Egyptian musician Sayed Darwish). For purposes of comparison,
the texts of both anthems are provided below in English translation.

Biladi, Biladi [6]

CHORUS
My homeland, my homeland, my homeland,
My love and my heart are for thee.
My homeland, my homeland, my homeland,
My love and my heart are for thee.

Egypt! O mother of all lands,
My hope and my ambition,
How can one count
The blessings of the Nile for mankind?

CHORUS
Egypt! Most precious jewel,
Shining on the brow of eternity!
O my homeland, be for ever free,
Safe from every foe!

CHORUS
Egypt! Noble are thy children,
Loyal, and guardians of thy soil.
In war and peace
We give our lives for thy sake.

CHORUS

This song exhibits qualities of a conventional national song with references to the spatial territory of the nation, descriptions of the exemplary role Egypt plays in world civilization as "mother of all lands," fervent calls for loyalty to the nation and to protect it from enemies, and the repeated proclamation of love for country. The song is free from sectarianism as there is no reference to any religious group.

"Illahi, Illahi" the alternative anthem, with the identical melody, rhythm, and cadence of *"Biladi, Biladi,"* carries an undeniably more subversive, revolutionary, content.

Illahi, Illahi

(refrain)
My God, My God, My God,
You're my strength, you're my wealth.

Brothers, let's establish
A state of the straight religion.
My call is not and will not be mild,
I rely upon God.

My brothers who are the martyrs,
Who want paradise,
His way is very hard.
I rely upon God.

My brothers, let's reestablish
The state of glorious truth,
A state of straight religion.
My call is not and will not be mild.

And proclaim "God is great!"
So it shocks the non-believers and they flee.
So proclaim "God is great!"
And glorify that God.

The religious anthem, *Illahi, Illahi,* projects an undeniably revolutionary tone that includes the rhetoric of martyrdom invocative of a language of *jihad,* as illustrated in the lines: "My call is not and will not be mild" and "My brothers who are the martyrs, Who want paradise, His way is very hard." It calls for an alternative state, one based presumably on *sharia* and Islamic principles as expressed in the line, "Brothers let's establish a state of the straight religion." It expresses a male-centeredness, as in its call to "brothers," but never "sisters," and a disdain for non-Muslims, as exemplified in the line, "and proclaim 'God is great! So it shocks the non-believers and they flee." The anthem's content is highly problematical when we consider that this ritual is supposed to instill in students an identification with, and loyalty to, the nation. Whether or not this alternative anthem achieves its supposed aim of infusing the singer with a revolutionary feeling and inspiring him or her towards a path of martyrdom is an open, and to my mind, unanswerable questions.

What may be an even more significant aspect than the seditious content of this alternative anthem, is its form, an exact replica—with decidedly modified lyrics—of *"Biladi, Biladi."* The anthem holds evocative power specifically for members of the Egyptian nation, not for Muslims of other countries, and as such is infused with the very nationalist content—and even sentiment—that it attempts to subvert. Additionally, during the singing of the anthem, teachers use conventional disciplining techniques, common in other schools in the area, to ensure students maintain straight lines, refrain from fiddling and talking with each other, and sing the required lyrics. Teachers circulate the courtyard, sticks in hand, hitting or punching any student who was misbehaving.

By using and appropriating nationalist rituals, and by upholding repressive, violent discipline techniques typical of general schools in the surrounding area, the alternative order cultivated at Fatima School for Believers was limited at best. It may have fostered a feeling of opposition or distrust of the government—albeit while it was preparing students for success in the government education system—and it may have instilled Islamic dispositions, particularly in the realm of language. But rather than cultivating an alternative education grounded in political dissent and challenge to the status quo, the school seems to inculcate a culture of submission common to general schools in similar social and class environments.

The Commercialization of Islamic Schooling

As Islamic schooling reached the more socially affluent classes, it maintained some oppositional qualities but was practiced in considerably different ways. Schooling, insofar as it is a socializing organization, operates as a stratifying mechanism. A direct correlation exists between an individual's or group's affiliation with certain schools and their social status, and cultural, political and social capital (Bourdieu and Passeron 1977). The more desired and socially valued schools among the affluent urban middle class tend to be private language schools, which provide intensive second language training, usually in English, but also in French. Private Islamic language schools date to the mid-1980s (like other general language schools). They cater to parents who want their children to affirm their Islamic identity and acquire the credentials and training necessary to compete in the global marketplace. These schools endeavor to educate an economic elite grounded in the values of Islam.

In the 1980s, Islamic language schools (similar to general language schools) were usually set up as nonprofit organizations, educational cooperatives, or NGOs. Although profitable, they were not viewed primarily as lucrative business ventures, but as schools that offered high-quality education within an Islamic environment. With the economic liberalization of the 1990s, and subsequent proliferation of a new, more profit-driven private education market, investment schools (*madaris istathmariyya*) arrived on the education scene. Set up as investment companies, these schools were generally much more expensive, more luxurious, exclusive, isolated, and profit-oriented than their predecessors. Concentrated in the new, upscale urban communities on the outskirts of Cairo, their extensive grounds tend to include such luxury amenities as swimming pools, theatres, state-of-the-art science and computer labs, libraries, gyms, and cafeterias.

Critics from a range of political and ideological spectrums, as reflected in the range of newspapers, where they air their opinions, cautioned that the new education markets would lead to further educational and social disparities, and have called into question how the school boards of these schools, composed largely of business people, could make sound decisions relating to education. On the issue of Islamic investment schools, they have been especially harsh in accusing owners of commercializing Islam and profiting from the religious sentiment in society.

One high-end English language Islamic investment school, Paradise Gardens (a pseudonym), projects an image of cosmopolitan modernity. Established in 1994 by an Egyptian engineer who earned his graduate degree at an Egyptian national university, the school, built on nearly three thousand square meters, offers a "child-centered" approach to learning. Its grounds include large playgrounds, two mosques, small class sizes (with a maximum of twenty-three pupils), science laboratories, libraries, resource rooms, a swimming pool, a modern cafeteria, and ample sporting and extracurricular activities. Tuition is a hefty LE 8,000 for the first year and between LE 5,000 to LE 6,000 for subsequent years depending on the student's educational stage. Parents are also expected to pay a host of hidden fees throughout the year for a range of in-school and extracurricular activities, uniforms, and school services, which substantially increase the cost.

The school's elite cosmopolitan image is protected through the realm of language, clothing, food, facilities, and transport. The English language is an essential asset for success in the international business and scientific community and holds a central place in the school's program of studies. Great efforts are made to hire native English speakers, a sign of prestige for any language school. The student uniform is a British-style prep school uniform replete with a navy blue blazer with the school's insignia (two children, one male and one female, jumping in front of a rainbow), embroidered on the lapel. Girls from the preparatory stage have the option of wearing a white headscarf. The school's custom air-conditioned school buses are found in the well-to-do parts of Cairo, picking up and dropping off students. The school cafeteria offers lunch specials at the end of the week, which alternate between three American fast-food chains, McDonalds, Pizza Hut, and KFC. Finally, the school's showpiece is its computer lab, which is fully internet accessible and comes equipped with a full-time teacher, a young bearded man who wears a white prayer cap.

The school prides itself on its mission of raising Muslim children for the twenty-first century with equal attention to knowledge and faith. The school's primary goal, as stated in its bilingual Arabic English brochure (which has the school logo on the left hand side of the page, and an elaborate Arabic calligraphic drawing of "In the Name of Allah" on the right side, is to develop in its students "a personality committed to religious beliefs and values and, simultaneously, to follow up and take part in the rapid progress of science and technology." It also attempts to foster a spirit of transnational tolerance and calls on children to "respect . . . other cultures, beliefs and nationalities." Despite its stated commitment to tolerance and respect to others, similar to other Islamic schools, it strongly discourages non-Muslim students from enrolling in the school and, with rare exception, hires only Muslim staff. All the school's female teachers, including the only Christian English teacher, are required to purchase a staff uniform (from the school management), which consists of an ankle-length navy blue coat and long headscarf.

Islam permeates the everyday life of the school in a variety of ways. Fifteen minutes are devoted each morning to Quranic recitation and explanation. All the children participate in collective prayer, which is preceded by *dua'a*, the ritual cleansing before the prayer, and followed by a ten to fifteen minute religious discussion group in the mosque. At the primary level classes are mixed and girls and boys pray together, but from the preparatory stage they are separated in the mosque, the classroom, playground, and cafeteria. Class teachers are encouraged to incorporate religion in their lessons and to instruct children to greet each other with "*as-salamu aleykom*" and refer to each other as brother and sister. Teachers decorate their classrooms with religious posters in English and Arabic. Islam is also present in the realm of physical education and sports clubs. The school teams, or houses as they are called following the British system, are distinguished by color and name. Being an Islamic school, the houses are named after the Prophet Mohammad's four successors (*khulafa al-rashidun)* as follows: the blue team: Ali; the yellow team: Uthman; the red team: 'Umar; and the green team: Abou Bakr.

The school owner (a businessman by all accounts), sometimes invokes Islam as a justification to penalize teachers and dock their pay. The average teacher wage is LE 1000 per month, relatively high in relation to Arabic private schools, but low for a high-end language school that requires bilingual teachers. Rarely, however, do teachers receive their full month's pay. The owner, often invoking Islam, regularly docks a quarter day's pay for any number of minor infractions. A teacher who does not wear socks with her ankle length coat in the hot months, for example, is docked a quarter day's pay because, as the owner argues, socks are a requirement in Islam. Any number of arbitrary Islamic rules are applied, on the spot, to penalize teachers. One teacher explains that the owner runs the school with a businessman's sense of cost efficiency and uses whatever justification necessary—Islamic or otherwise—to cut costs and increase his own profit.[7] He plans to expand his business by opening a separate high school.

At Paradise Gardens, the management maximizes profit by charging high tuition fees, incorporating a host of hidden fees, and docking pay, from modest teacher salaries citing reasons of Islamic morality. The school, rather than working towards stated ideals of raising an elite Muslim generation grounded in values of respect, tolerance, and openness, appears more to be reinforcing notions of class privilege within an Islamic environment.

The Cultural Politics of School Uniforms

The debates on the various aspects of the Islamization of schooling focused heavily on female students. Muslim girls were thrust into the public spotlight when the issue of school uniforms became highly public and contentious. From the 1980's, schoolgirls—oftentimes as early as first grade—were increasingly required, by teachers and school administrators, to wear an Islamic uniform (al-ziyy al-Islami), which included a head covering of some sort. The Ministry of Education (MOE) reported receiving scores of complaints from around the country to the effect that Islamic uniforms were being imposed on girls.

From a legal perspective, educators were not violating government policy because the regulations guiding school uniforms—Ministerial Orders #70 of 1962 and #139 of 1981—did not explicitly forbid Islamic uniforms. In 1994, the MOE issued revised legislation on school uniforms, Ministerial Order 113, of 1994, on the Unification of School Uniforms, which forbids girls in primary school from covering their hair and requires that girls in the preparatory stage, who wear a headscarf, provide written permission from a guardian, thereby giving parents, rather than school authorities, the right to decide what their daughters should wear (implying that adolescent girls themselves are not yet at an age to exert free choice over their actions). The Order prohibits the niqab, the full face veil, at all educational levels.

The Minister encountered an onslaught of criticism from different ideological camps for interfering in the religious, moral, and cultural practices of individuals and schools. The opposition press reported numerous stories from the perspective of ordinary Egyptians relating their feelings of injustice and helplessness in the face of a heavy-handed state that intruded into their private lives. One father, on being told by a school principal that his primary school daughters would not be allowed in their school until they removed their head-scarves, replied:

> How can I ask my daughters, whom I want to raise in accordance with God's satisfaction, to take off the *hijab*? I am a simple Muslim and I don't belong to any extremist organization or even a [political] party. I just try to follow the instructions of our religion, the first of which is to raise my children in a proper Islamic way. (Al-Shaab, 1994).

In a campaign to gain public support for his highly controversial uniform policy, Baha Eddin pursued a strategy that combined religious doctrine with scientific reasoning. He capitalized on his position as an educated Muslim by frequently quoting the Quran and making references to the *sunnah* and *hadith* (examples and sayings of the Prophet Mohammad). He equally drew on his authority as a medical doctor by citing evidence from psychology, education science, and medicine, to justify his position. He rallied the support of strategic religious figures, including the Grand Mufti and Shaykh of al-Azhar, Muhammad Sayed Tantawi, who issued a *fatwa* (religious ruling) stating that the *niqab* is not a requirement in Islam. Tantawi went even further by vouching for the Minister's religious integrity by characterizing him as "a strong Muslim [who] has organized thinking and...would not issue a decision which violates the Islamic sharia" (Al-Ahram 1994).

Despite the Azhar's support, the uniform legislation triggered enormous public debate and resulted in a spate of lawsuits. Some parents sued for the right of their primary school daughters to wear the *hijab*, while others disputed the *niqab* ban. The well-known Islamist lawyer, Montasser al-Zayyat, tried and won over twenty-five *niqab*-related cases in the lower courts. Finally, in a 1996 appeal that reached the Supreme Constitutional Court—Egypt's highest court—Ministerial Order 113 of 1994 was ruled constitutional. Even so, Islamic dress in educational and other settings remains a highly divisive issue and new disputes continuously appear in the courts. The cultural politics that have emerged around the issue of school uniforms allow for an inquiry into youth agency and the ways in which youth practices can influence school environments towards greater plurality of practice.

"The School of the Faithful" (a pseudonym), a private Islamic school located in a middle-class, professional area of Cairo, was founded on the familiar principles that Muslim children should receive their basic education in an atmosphere of simplicity, piety, and charity, and should be guarded from the adverse influences of materialism, secularism, and Western cultural encroachment. Its founder, Shaykh Mohammed, a former functionary at the Ministry of Religious Endowments (MRE), set as the school's main objectives that children master the Quran and the Arabic language, comport themselves in a decent, religiously sanctioned manner, and avoid activities that distract them from their religion. Along these lines, the coeducational school's formal policies include sex segregation of students (boys and girls use separate stairways, playgrounds, and classrooms), mandatory extracurricular Quran classes, and a mandatory Islamic uniform for female students and teachers.

When the school opened in 1981, the school uniform for girls from the first grade consisted of a long white scarf that covered the chest and torso known as a *khimar,* and an ankle-length gray smock. In 1994, following the new ministerial order on school uniforms, the school's uniform policy changed; the headscarf was eliminated for girls at the primary level and, with 100 percent cooperation of parents who agreed to sign the required consent form, the *hijab* remained mandatory for girls at the preparatory stage.

Shaykh Mohammed did not initially agree to changing his school's uniform, but was forced to do so as a result of the heavy surveillance of private Islamic schools. Inspectors and state security personnel were dispatched to schools throughout the country and in many cases blocked students in defiance of the new uniform regulation from entering their schools. At a private Islamic school in a similar professional middle-class neighborhood, tensions rose as students witnessed schoolmates being harassed by state security guards. A student, who at that time was fourteen years-old, recalled vividly her outrage at seeing her schoolmates being treated like criminals:

> Officials from the government came to our school and stood at the door saying that any primary school students wearing the scarf wouldn't be allowed to enter. They were asking girls to take off their scarves at the gate. The rest of us were standing in line for the *tabour* and were aware of girls being kept out of school. We all went to the corridor and sat down blocking the way and said we wouldn't move until the girls were allowed in. We started shouting out in unison, *La Illah ila Allah* (there is no God but God) until they agreed to let them in. Our class started it. We sat on the floor and other classes joined us.

We were all very upset. The next day we made signs saying: 'you cannot force anyone to disobey God.' If God is telling you to do something, no one can convince you otherwise, not even your mother and father. All of us students were involved in this and we encouraged each other. The teachers also got involved. Even the girls who didn't used to wear the *hijab* came to school the next day wearing it. We wrote slogans on the walls and encouraged each other to wear the *hijab*.

Many students and staff felt a sense of indignation against the government for what they considered an unjust interference into the internal policy of their schools. In an act of defiance, some members of school communities, as the students described above, more firmly exhibited an outward commitment to Islam. In the School of the Faithful, it was no different. Many students and staff initially criticized the uniform regulation. However, many students, followed by a growing number of staff, began modifying their style of dress in a gradual process of what can be called "downveiling" (Herrera 2000; 2001). With the backing of the new uniform regulation, and with the cover of constant government inspectors, the older girls at the school aged twelve- to fourteen-years-old, substituted their uniform *khimar* for a simple white scarf and, in an act of noncooperation against school policy, decided among themselves to replace the regulation gray smock which they described as ugly and old-fashioned (*balady*) for a more "normal" and attractive uniform of a tailored, long gray skirt and white blouse. While the downveiling of adolescent girls might be explained to some extent by their interest in youth fashion, their desire to appear more attractive, or as exhibiting a spirit of rebellion against school authorities, these reasons do not explain why, over the succeeding years, many of the school staff, aged between their late twenties and early fifties, also began downveiling.

The most high-profile adult downveilers were two senior administrators, second in command only to the principal. These in-school disciplinarians gradually substituted their dark ankle-length skirts for slightly shorter cotton skirts and, in gradations, replaced their thick polyester *khimars*, for shoulder-length cotton scarves. Both women had begun wearing the *khimar* just prior to being employed at the school in the early 1980s, in part to demonstrate their commitment to working in an Islamic environment. When the primary school girls ceased to cover their hair, and when the girls at the preparatory level downveiled to much simpler and lighter forms of clothing, the need to dress religiously on par with the students no longer existed.

In conversations with other teachers who downveiled, it seemed that they did so largely in the interest of comfort and functionality, not as the result of a lessening of their piety or less commitment to identifying with an Islamic lifestyle. Some women explained that the tight nylon *khimar* caused their hair to thin—in some cases lead to their getting bald patches—so they substituted it for a looser-fitting cotton scarf. Other women, who routinely walked long distances to and from work, complained that the *khimar*, while perhaps religiously preferable to the *hijab*, proved too cumbersome and caused them to perspire excessively. Some unmarried *niqab* wearers (*munaqqabat*) removed the face cover because they felt their prospects for marriage were diminished when suitors could not see their faces. Many of the women who downveiled were quick to express a degree of regret in doing so, and pointed out that despite their current practice, more conservative and concealing forms of dress were preferable. They often pointed to some undisclosed time in the future when they might take up a more correct and pious form of dress.

The students in the upper grades clearly had the effect of relaxing the dress code among the school staff and in redefining—through a process of questioning and experimenting—norms around what constituted acceptable attire. This is not to say that dress and comportment did not remain the subject of much scrutiny from all sides, it did. Teachers, including the downveilers, continued to supervise and discipline girls for any number of infractions such as buttoning their blouses too low, wearing their skirts too short or too tight, or going "too far" in their grooming or dress choices. The parameters of what constituted too far underwent flux, as did the students' readiness to accept their teachers' moral authority. A seventh-grade student remarked, "Our school has really changed. In the beginning it was very strict and all our teachers wore the *khimar* or the *niqab*. Now [some of those same teachers] wear tight clothes with a little scarf." To which her friend added, "a very, very little scarf." An eighth-grade girl complained that the vice principal scolded her for wearing a uniform skirt that fit too snugly around her hips and asked, "How can she comment on my appearance when she herself used to wear the *khimar*, took it off, and now only wears a scarf? She tells us not to wear tight clothing but she sometimes wears very tight skirts with sandals." As the choices about correct comportment, fashion, and morality widened, students struggled among themselves to come to terms with their own choices, as evidenced in an exchange by two seventh-grade girls:

Girl One: You see lots of people these days walking in the street with a scarf and tight pants or stretch pants. Pants, anyway, are *haram* (Islamically forbidden) for girls.

Girl Two: But you yourself wear pants, and stretch pants at that.

Girl One: I do, but I'm not veiled. I don't wear a scarf. I'm talking about people who have made the decision to wear the scarf and still wear tight pants. People say that it's *haram* for the woman who wears a scarf to also wear pants.

Girl Two: Look, I'm not veiled either, but I don't wear stretch pants and low-cut blouses that expose my chest. I'll wear a blouse, a skirt, something like that. Even girls who don't wear the *hijab* should still be modest about how they dress.

As the dress and broader lifestyle choices of students and staff shifted and broadened in response to a host of factors, young women expressed ambiguity over who in society holds the moral authority to decide what is correct behavior. They continuously evaluate how to cope with the messages and choices available to them from a range of moral influences, including mass media, the government, religious authorities, formal educators, and peers. This is reflected in an exchange between two eighth-grade girls:

Girl One: People these days are saying that all kinds of things are haram: television is haram, cucumbers are haram, sausages are haram, Johnson Shampoo is haram. The Shaykhs should be the only ones who say what is haram and not the people, because they invent weird things.

Girl Two: In the old times people had to explain where they got their information about what is haram. Today anyone can say anything is haram, and we don't know the source. You shouldn't believe everything you hear.

While in the mid-to-late-1990s, the school could be said to have experienced a movement towards downveiling, some students and staff have more recently exhibited signs of "upveiling" by adapting more conservative and concealing forms of dress. This latter trend seems to have occurred in part as a response— advanced through a growing Islamic print, electronic, and audiovisual media—to dissatisfaction with national politics, combined with a defensive piety that has arisen in response to aggressive attacks on Muslim majority states such as Iraq, Afghanistan, and Palestine.

I do not mean to infer that the act of downveiling, or the choice by women to wear less concealing forms of clothing, implies a necessary movement towards what might be called female emancipation, or that upveiling represents an opposite trend.[8] I do not regard the degree to which a woman covers or exposes her body as an a priori indication of the extent of her agency or freedom of choice. With some caveats, both forced veiling (such as in Iran and Saudi Arabia), and forced *unveiling* (as in France and Turkey), can deny the right of women to make mature rational choices. Rather, my interest in looking at processes of downveiling and upveiling, is an attempt to understand how social groups, in this case female youths, critically reflect on and engage in their environment in ways that lead them to question norms and power, and act in ways that can lead to greater plurality of practices and ideas.

Youth, Agency, and Education

Islamists, businesspersons, and young women, have been influencing practices and processes of Islamic schooling. Members and sympathizers of Islamist movements sometimes use Islamic schools to promote an alternative political agenda while reinforcing authoritarian cultures. As a response to economic opportunities arising from neoliberal privatizing reforms, members of the business sector tapped into a new Islamic school market for the upper middle classes. Rather than working towards stated ideals of raising an elite Muslim generation grounded in values of respect, tolerance, and openness, they appear more to be reinforcing notions of class privilege within a seeming rigid Islamic environment.

As the cultural politics of school uniforms demonstrates, Islamic schooling produced unanticipated effects on adolescent middle-class female students who, by being the objects of different policies and ideologies, took certain matters into their own hands. Their actions included staging sit-ins to protest the heavy-handed security tactics used against their schoolmates; challenging the Ministry of Education through court cases and other means; overriding their school authorities by changing their own school uniforms; and constantly questioning and discussing issues around who has legitimate moral and religious authority to make decisions about how they should comport themselves. They made active choices based on processes of observing, questioning, and reflecting about what is fair and right. These young women contributed to an opening of their school cultures towards more questioning and pluralism of ideas and practice. Educators interested in facilitating and realizing a more open and active Islamic education would do well to listen to the concerns of youth, give credence to the ways in which they understand and critically interact with their environment, and facilitate their searches for ways to make choices about how to live in and act on the world.

Notes to Chapter 1

1. Unless otherwise indicated, all translations from Arabic to English are my own.

2. The late Dr. Galal's report was reported in Egypt's semigovernmental weekly magazine *Roz al Youssef* (1993). Unable to obtain the original report, the author discussed the findings with his colleagues from MOE in 1999.

3. In the 1992-1993 scholastic year for example, the Supreme Council for Education allocated LE 4.5 million toward social services which benefited roughly 150,000 university students, increased its student housing capacity to 56,000, and expanded government-sponsored summer camps for university students. In 1992-1993 7,500 students partook in camps organized and subsidized by Egyptian universities in resorts south of Cairo in Helwan and on the Mediterranean coast in Alexandria. The government-sponsored camps, similar to the Islamists camps, included symposia on social issues and thereby served an ideological as well as a social or recreational function (National Center for Educational Research and Development 1994, 44).

4. Information regarding extremist teachers reaches the Ministry through three basic venues: parents who convey their grievances through letters or personal visits to educational authorities; the press which summarily reports pedagogical

and curricular breaches at schools; and local district inspectors who make regular supervisory visits to schools.

5. Statistics on private Islamic schools have been compiled by the author.

6. This translation has been taken from the website http://www.egyptvoyager.com/features_anthem.htm and was downloaded on 8 May 2004.

7. Interview with a teacher from the school on March 19, 2002 in Cairo.

8. There are those who argue that in some cases veiling represents a form of women's liberation (El Guindi 1999), and others who argue that questions around veiling in Europe and North America can reflect crises in liberalism (Herrera and Moors 2003).

References

Abdalla, Ahmed. 1985. *The Student Movement and National Politics in Egypt: 1923-1973.* London: Al Saqi Books.

Abdelrahman, Maha. 2005. *Civil Society Exposed: The Politics of NGOs in Egypt.* London: I .B. Taurus.

Akhbar al Hawadith. 1993. "The Complete Plan for Confronting the Network of Extremists in the Education Sector" (in Arabic) 13 May.

Al-Ahram. 1993. "The Minister of Education demands the participation of education professors in developing education, bringing up youngsters and abolishing terrorism" (in Arabic), 26 April, 10.

Al-Ahram. 1994. "The Decision of the Hijab: The Mufti of Al-Azhar supports it" (in *Al-Hayat.* 1995. "Hussein Kamal Baha Eddin: Eliminating Extremist Teachers is an Urgent Measure but the Real Solution is to Develop the Curriculum" (in Arabic), 17.

Al-Shaab. (Cairo) 1994. Disputing the Minister of Education's Decision for Forbidding the Hijab as an Obligatory Duty. 31 October.

Arab Republic of Egypt. 1994. *Ministerial Decision 113 for 1994* (in Arabic). Cairo: Ministry of Education.

Baha Eddin, Husayn Kamal. 1997. *Al-Ta'lim wa al-mustaqbal (Education and the Future)* (in Arabic), Cairo: Dar al-Ma`arif.

Bourdieu, Pierre, and Jean-Claude Passeron. 1977. *Reproduction in Education, Society, and Culture.* London: Sage.

Cairo Times. 2004. Extreme Education. March 18024, 7.

Eickelman, Dale, and Jon Anderson. 1999. *New Media in the Muslim World: The Emerging Public Sphere.* Indiana University Press.

El Guindi, Fadwa. 1999. *Veil: Modesty, Privacy and Resistance.* Oxford and New York: Berg.

Esposito, John L. 2003. Islam and civil society. In *Modernizing Islam: Religion in the Public Sphere in Europe and the Middle East,* ed. John L. Esposito and François Burgat, 69–100. London: Hurst.

Herrera, Linda. 1992. Scenes of schooling: Inside a girls' school in Cairo. *Cairo Papers in Social Science* 15 (1).

———. 2000. Downveiling: Shifting socioreligious practices in Egypt. *ISIM Newsletter,* no. 6: 1 & 32.

———. 2001. Downveiling: Gender and the contest over culture in Egypt. *Middle East Report,* no. 219: 16–19.

———. December, 2003. with Annelies Moors. Banning face veiling: The boundaries of liberal education. *ISIM Newsletter* no.13 (of the International Institute for the Study of Islam in the Modern World), p. 16–17. (http://www.isim.nl/files/newsl_13–16.pdf).

Human Rights Watch. 2005. Reading between the "Red Lines": The repression of academic freedom in Egyptian universities. Vol. 17 (6).

Kandil, Amani. 1998. The nonprofit sector in Egypt. In *The nonprofit sector in the developing world: A comparative analysis,* ed. Helmut K. Anheier and Lester M. Salamon. Manchester: Manchester University Press.

Kienle, Eberhard. 2001. *A Grand delusion: Democracy and economic reform in Egypt.* London and New York: I. B. Tauris Publishers.

Maughith, Kamal. 1998. Religious education between tolerance and violence [in Arabic]. Paper presented at conference of the Upper Egyptian Society, May 19–20.

Middle East Times. (Cairo) 1995. Militants expelled from schools. 1 and 16.

National Centre for Educational Research and Development (NCERD). (1994). *Development of Education in Arab Republic of Egypt 92/1993–93/1994.* Cairo: National Centre for Educational Research and Development.

Norton, Augustus. R., ed. 1995. *Civil society in the Middle East.* Vol. 1. Leiden: E. J. Brill.

October. 1993. The minister of education answers the extremists [in Arabic]. 2 May.

Roz al Yousif. 1993. Teachers wanted for capital punishment [in Arabic], 10 May, 26–28.

Salvatore, Armando. 1999. *Islam and the public discourse of modernity.* Ithaca, NY: Ithaca Press.

Starrett, Gregory. 1998. *Putting Islam to work: Education, politics and religious transformation in Egypt.* Berkeley: University of California Press.

Sullivan D. 1994. *Voluntary associations in Egypt.* University Press of Florida.

2

The Production and Reproduction of Culture in Egyptian Schools

KAMAL NAGUIB

Summary

The cultural production of individuals who pass through the schooling process represents a highly neglected area of research and inquiry. The present study, an ethnographic investigation of ten public sector schools, places particular attention on processes of cultural reproduction and production and the strategies students and teachers employ to resist forms of power and control. Critical ethnographers try to determine complex social processes that occur between the school culture and the culture of the macrosociety by assuming that the microculture of the school reflects a microcosm of society and an element of social production. Through the ethnographic approach, the author demonstrates how the authoritarian nature of the Egyptian state is reflected in an authoritarian culture of schooling. Due to its cumbersome and hierarchical bureaucratic structure, schools tend to reproduce a culture of surrender, dishonesty, and hopelessness. The result has partly been the production of new youth cultures in which distrust and violence play central roles. The author grapples with how to change an emerging cycle of oppression and violence in schools.

Towards a Critical Sociology of Arab Education

> Any nation, whose people, or most of its people, do not feel the suffering caused by despotism, does not deserve its freedom.
> —'Abd al-Rahman al-Kawakibi, *The Nature of Despotism and the Struggle of the Enslaved*

53

> Any actual change in a given society can only emerge from
> within the depth of that society (i.e., by a transformation of its
> essence). For true liberation can only occur through a movement
> that is born from the heart of a society (i.e., self-liberation).
> —Hisham Sharabi, *Introduction to a Study of Arab Society*

The cultural production of individuals who pass through the schooling process represents a highly neglected area of research and inquiry. The
present study, an ethnographic investigation of Egyptian classroom culture, places particular attention on processes of cultural reproduction and
production and the strategies students and teachers employ to resist forms
of power and control. Critical ethnographers try to determine complex
social processes that occur between the school culture and the culture of
the macrosociety by assuming that the microculture of the school reflects
a microcosm of society and an element of social production.[1]

In his seminal work, *Learning to Labour*, Paul Willis makes a persua-
sive case for the use of qualitative methodologies in critical education
research. He argues that the survey and questionnaire (standard tools of
the Arab social sciences) simply do not "have the depth to report and
show the creative life of cultures," and posits that "'cultural forms' and
movements can only be researched in a *valid* way by direct forms of
fieldwork" (1981, 218). This study, following the lead of not only Willis,
but a generation of critical educationists, is grounded in the premise that
qualitative methodologies provide the most discerning way to study the
dynamics, forms, and processes of cultural production. The ethnographic approach, which necessitates using diverse research tools including participant observation, interviews, and the critical interpretation of
primary and secondary sources, allows for an intimate analytical description of the daily reality of schools within the macrosocial structures of a
given society.[2] The microculture of schools, as the Arab scholar Abd al-
Sami Sayyid Ahmed so concisely states, reflects "both an extension of
society's culture and a factor of its production" (1990, 83).

Despite the arrival of a critical movement in the field of pedagogy in
Egypt in the 1980s,[3] and despite the growing recognition of the necessity
of qualitative research in the sociology of education, one is hard-pressed
to find even the remotest sign of these developments in the Arabic literature (for some exceptions see the Introduction).[4] Strangely enough, even
though the field of modern educational studies in Egypt dates to the
mid-nineteenth century (influenced by models from North America and

Europe), it has not been accompanied by any corresponding interest in analyzing the effects of educational processes on daily social activities. In fact, the sociology of education is a highly underdeveloped field in the Arab world. The few Arabic studies from the region are limited to a treatment of megatheories, originating in the West, that explain how mass schooling is linked to macro-socioeconomic and political institutions. Given the restrictive research climates and impediments to critical researchers in many Arab states, one can understand how it would not be very rewarding for researchers to consume new theories without being able to test their validity in local contexts, or at least benefit from comparing local cases with other cases. Researchers, reformers, and educational practitioners in the Arab world may justifiably be wary of mechanically applying CST perspectives developed in other contexts for fear that they can be misleading and might not contribute to understanding local realities or to solving its problems. Yet critical qualitative analyses, when adapted to the conditions of local environments, can provide us with a much-needed basis to test the validity and assess the degree of reliability of contemporary critical theories and inform us about the Egyptian educational environment (Al-Bialawi 1986,1990). Any discussion on classroom culture in Egyptian schools, finally, must include a discourse on both despotism and liberty.

School Environments

Having obtained the necessary and extremely hard-to-attain permits to conduct ethnographic studies of public schools in Egypt, preparations and activities for this study took place over the course of nine months, from September 2002–May 2003. The sample study was composed of fifty-four students (both sexes), forty teachers (both sexes), and twenty directors, principals, and vice principals from ten schools (both sexes) in the city of Alexandria. The researcher's initial objective was to identify the features of school culture in low-income public-sector preparatory schools (grades 6–8), and to understand the values, traditions, dynamics, and social relations that characterize student and teacher interactions inside and outside the classroom. These observations would then allow for an analysis of both processes of control and processes of cultural production and resistance, otherwise called counterculture or culture of resistance.

The main research question motivating the study is: "What are the norms or features of the dominant culture and counterculture present in Egyptian preparatory schools and classrooms?" The secondary questions, linked to the main question, are as follows:

- What social patterns and social organization are prevalent in Egyptian preparatory schools and classrooms?
- What dominant values and traditions rule the social organization of schooling?
- What is the nature of the social relationship between administrators and teachers?
- How are workloads and responsibilities distributed among school administrations?
- How is work distributed between teachers and students inside the classroom?
- What are the prevailing principles that govern the social organization of educational processes, and to what extent do teacher-student interactions reflect principles of equity and fairness?
- What are the customary teaching methods?
- What are the degrees of student participation inside classrooms?
- What are the norms that govern behavior between students, teachers, and of both groups with the administration?

With regard to issues of control and resistance, the questions posed are:

- What are the norms and patterns of school order and student discipline?
- What are the various forms of cultural production and to what extent do students resist the dominant culture inside the classroom?
- How do teachers handle forms of resistance?

The research techniques used to address these questions include in-depth field observation, participant observation, and individual and focus group interviews. Through systematic observation of students' discussions, their modes of recreation, participation in school and daily activities, and their study habits, the researcher identified prevailing diverse modes of cultural production. I made over thirty classroom visits, conducted some of the classes myself, and participated in extracurricular classes and recreational activities. This level of engagement allowed me to understand individual students' normative responses to each other, to their teachers, as well as their group responses to school authorities. I conducted in-depth interviews with twenty directors, headmasters, vice principals, forty teachers, and fifty-four students. The subjects were both male and female. The interviews allowed for discussions on issues ranging from social relations within the school, discipline, and responses to official regulations, school rituals, and school problems, perceptions of different issues of curricula and teaching, and their suggestions for improvement. Focus group meetings with students and teachers allowed for further discussions on issues formerly raised.

All the schools in this study were single-sex preparatory level schools located in the district of Alexandria; they included five girls' schools and five boys' schools. The ten sample schools represent a unified social and pedagogical community on the one hand, and are set apart by certain distinguishing features, the most notable being social class, on the other hand. Of the ten schools, seven were located in working-class or impoverished shantytown areas, and three were located in more affluent urban middle class areas. According to an admission policy followed in the city of Alexandria called "connectivity," in which students graduating from specific elementary schools must continue their preparatory schooling in specifically assigned schools, all the schools admit students from poor areas.

In addition to growing poverty in poor urban and slum areas, other factors contribute to the adverse cultural and social conditions of the populations of these areas. Factors such as increasing illiteracy rates, deterioration of the level of education of the civic community combined with a lack of cultural life, dominance of provincial rural customs, harsh social conditions, and the deterioration of the physical environment, represent just some of the challenges these communities face. All these factors foster particular forms of social and cultural behavior that penetrate the school environment.

With regard to the school facilities, their physical conditions varied. Half the schools were built according to a standard pre-designed mold by the Organization for the Construction of Educational Facilities (a two-story, L-shaped concrete structure facing an open courtyard). By and large, these schools could not accommodate the school community and lacked space for required facilities such as teachers' rooms, communal halls, administrative offices, school yards (too narrow), and educational laboratories. The other five schools were originally old villas converted into schools, one of which dated to the nineteenth century and the others to the 1950s and 1960s. They were in relatively better condition than the newer schools and were more spacious. One of the aims of this study is to analyze how the local environment influences the particular school culture and students' cultural expressions.

The Pyramidal Hierarchy of School Culture

Schools are organized according to an elaborate, pyramidal, authoritarian hierarchy that places each member vertically above the other, and horizontally with each one against the other. The school administrative board is composed of one managing director followed by an ordinary director of lower rank, one or more headmasters, and a row of vice principals organized by seniority: first rank teachers and, finally, teachers and students. Each school contains about fifteen senior administrators, yet there is no functional justification for this packed administrative pyramid that represents the essence of power of the school. Many senior administrators simply wait at their desks for orders or instructions from school directors. One director described this pyramidal structure as "an unsuccessful system that allows for the confusion of job roles." The system also leads to unfairness in the distribution of tasks because the bulk of responsibilities, as the same director pointed out, "all rests on number one." This type of administrative pyramid is replicated in almost all work environments in Egypt, a society that preserves and values honorific titles and ranks more than work and performance. The elaborate hierarchies in the workplace and in schools are not designed to facilitate the management processes, but to reproduce symbols of authority and relations of control and submission.

Since the responsibility falls on number one—the head director (*al-mudir(a)*)—he/she becomes the axis around which all school affairs are centered; he/she is also the axis of discipline and control. Since the director is in the top position of responsibility, her/his authority is absolute, and as such he/she demands total obedience and submission from all subordinates. The essential structure of relationships at schools are founded on the principle of "monopoly of sources of power and authority," employed for the benefit of the bureaucratic higher powers. Yet the director's authority and areas of jurisdiction are contained by the instructions and memorandums of the upper administrative authorities.

School organization is structured in such a way that it does not promote participation from its employees in any manner, whether from members of the administrative board, like headmasters and vice principals, or from teachers and students. In fact, this top-down structural arrangement actually leads to a transgression of rights, jurisdiction, and responsibilities, and deprives school administrators of their authority. It also impedes their attempts to improve their professional and administrative performance. Finally, this hierarchical culture breeds problems and hinders performance by turning educators into administrators with no power of recourse to effect change. The matter therefore goes beyond the normal definitions of employer and employee; it transforms itself into the mindset of oppressor and oppressed. The school workers, whether belonging to the administrative rung or the teaching rung, learn how not to do their original work as directors or teachers; instead they learn how to comply with the instructions and regulations of the head directors or to the regulations and decrees of higher administrative authorities.

Despotism by Proxy

The Egyptian education system is made up of three major pyramids: (1) the administrative board located in the schools, (2) the local education district or governorate (*mudariyya*), and (3) the Ministry of Education, the great pyramid of central authority. Each pyramid contains successively smaller pyramids consisting of units of technical inspection, local and central supervisory committees, financial and administrative inspectors, preparatory level educational boards, directors of different educational stages, department heads, and curricula inspectors. Within each section are multiple authorities who work for a higher authority and implement the instructions, directives, and educational decisions of that authority. Directives are implemented according to the understandings and interpretative capacities of the individuals in charge.

Even though school directors hold substantial power in their schools, they are subject to continuous monitoring and supervision from the outside; their work is regulated by ministerial orders pertaining to every minute detail of their work. The relationship between the smaller school pyramid and the bigger pyramids is based on the use of violence, coercion, and suppression. Punishment and harsh penalties are the fate of dissenting directors who fail to implement the higher ups' regulations and instructions. Yet instructions are often full of contradictions and discrepancies, leaving school directors unsure of how to implement them. As one director complains:

> The funny thing is that the upper administration just does not understand anything it is doing! It sends you these contradictory instructions and contradictory memos. One memo tells you the school sponsored private lessons (*majmuaat*) should be given on a voluntarily basis and the school should not put pressure on students to take these lessons. At the same time, if too few students take these lessons they take me to task and deduce [unjustly] that we are in [secret] agreements with teachers to promote private lessons outside the school. We're supposed to control the students, but there is no control. We have to admit students to class no matter how late they arrive. They have tied my hands and feet and have thrown me out to sea. They have left me there and I don't know how to get to the shore.

The power and authority to "command and forbid" resides only with those located at the upper levels of the great pyramids, especially with the one who sits on top of the greatest pyramid commanding absolute obedience (i.e., the Minister). The smaller pyramids that exist at the level of the school have no power whatsoever, and their top executives are helpless; some even consider it a form of punishment to be promoted to the position of school director, as one director so caustically sums up:

> Each time we are promoted we are actually demoted since each promotion includes a loss of dignity. You will find, for example, that the school director has a rank of managing director while the supervisors and inspectors who examine the school belong to a lower rank. How could that be? Besides, this inspection and supervisory system is a total failure! When school directors commit infractions, they're removed from their office and get appointed to the supervisory committees. They are not fit to supervise. Anyone without work in the Ministry becomes a supervisor.

He continues to describe how the system of inspection disrupts the educational process and patently fails to achieve its intended goals of improving the quality or efficiency of the education system:

About seven to eight supervisors come to the school on a daily basis. Not only are they useless, but they obstruct the schooling process. They blame the director for anything that goes wrong. If there are any deficits, the director is responsible; low exam grades, the director is responsible; low attendance, the director is again responsible. Shall I get a minivan and pick up students from their homes?! No one wants to be promoted to the post of school director because they are responsible for everything and have no authority whatsoever!

Another school director complains:

I'm responsible for anything that happens in the school, no one else. This keeps me on edge all the time and I'm a bundle of nerves. This school has thirty-four hundred students, in other words thirty-four hundred landmines capable of exploding any time

Hierarchical administrative structures located both inside and outside schools have transformed administrators into individuals with no power or authority. Their helplessness translates into a sense of impotence and grows into a fear of making mistakes. The constant threat of punishment leads people to take the safe path; in order to avoid conflict and retribution they may resort to lies, hypocrisy, and flattery. Those in lower administrative ranks present a false rosy picture of school life under their control, and systematically cover-up any problems. A school director explains their dilemma:

We are a people who are full of fear. We do not tell the truth. Our problem is that we allow the lower ones to cheat us. They always tell me, 'all is fine boss'...Why? Because they are all afraid of retribution. Our problem is that we are hypocrites who do not speak honestly.

The harsh penal structure reproduces an even more intensive degree of fear and submission at the level of the relationship between school administration and upper administrative authorities. The director of another school relates:

I am a school director. I have three sons, all of whom are in university. I graduated from the university in 1972 and my current salary is [a mere] 500 LE....I had to make my wife work and we just make ends meet. If I utter just one word [of complaint] they would throw me out. If I make trouble with that one, or object to another one, I will simply expose myself to the probability of a transfer. You ask me about 'democratic government,' well I want to tell you something. I swear by God, by God in front of the other directors, that I am afraid to pronounce his name [the name of Minister]. I am too afraid to pronounce it lest I be humiliated. Shall we kid each other? There is neither democracy nor anything else here.

Imagine the extent of fear and panic directors feel when they cannot even utter aloud the name of a known official in public! Naturally directors train themselves through their repeated dealings with members of the upper administrative authorities to refrain both from criticizing the system and offering ideas for improvement. Directors learn to suppress their aggression towards the despotic power and to avoid any confrontation with it. This leads them to acquiescence, submission, passivity, lying, and hypocrisy. A school may be poorly run and disorderly all year-round, however, on the days of official visits, directors would see to it that the school runs in an orderly manner.

The dealings of senior administrators with their subordinates, whether from the lower echelons of the administration or from the staff, predictably reflect an entirely different power dynamic. As described by one director, young schoolteachers are "careless, passive...some of them are without any integrity and they only respond to coercion." Therefore, it is not surprising that teachers recounted many stories about unfair treatment and oppression at the hands of school administrators. They were especially critical about how administrators based rewards and punishments on personal relations. One teacher explains:

> The school director punished a teacher because he forgot to write the date in his draft notebook. He deducted three days of his pay. Why? The director was personally upset with the teacher. When my colleague is wrongly punished the whole lot of us are also oppressed.

As for their views on students, directors prefer to nurture fear rather than love or respect, as one director explains: "this [young] age needs fear more than love. There is not sufficient time for all of that." On a similar note another director notes:

> Our kids need to be toughened up and [made to] bear responsibility. The kids of today are spoilt and do not want to be educated. They have aggressive, destructive tendencies. They need a prison specialist. In the old days, there used to be a security officer at schools with direct contact to the police. He would take any delinquent students to the police station where they would get what they deserved. Then they would come back to school set straight. Such a prison specialist is needed in our schools today.

The notion that a school could only function properly if run with an iron fist and that students could only be kept in line with the tactics of a prison specialist, reflect a breakdown of social cohesion. The façade of cohesion lasts only as long as the directors are present. Observations have clearly confirmed that schools fall into a state of chaos and disorder when directors are not present—just as schools are poorly run until an important delegation comes to make a visit. We can say that the director represents a symbol, or formal façade of customs and norms of behavior. Methods of monitoring, supervision, and inspection, as well as harsh penal codes, play a major role in defining and molding the relationship between school directors and upper administrative powers into a despotism that is very close to a master/slave relationship. This means that the director can only be a director once he/she has perfected the art of suppression and submission within her/his administrative jurisdiction (similar to the role of a prison warden).

Egyptian schools today are operating in an age of despotic directors who alternate between the role of master and slave. Directors reproduce the logic of authoritarianism that permeates sociopolitical life in Egypt. The government authority coerces citizens into submission in the name of the law, whereas directors force school employees into submission in the name of their official position. Both represent a power derived from laws and legislation.[5] What this means is that school directors are not directors in any real sense of the word since they do not, and cannot direct. Rather, they execute decisions and regulations that are continuously issued to them from above and which predetermine the contours of what is permissible and forbidden, what has to be done and what should not be done, and which impose on them a silence and play-dead role. Thus, directors' despotism is actually a despotism by proxy; they are agents of despotism in compliance to, and as an expression of, the desires of the higher authority and its good. Thus, we find directors as individuals disappearing under the cover of their job title, and in turn, the job title disappears under the cover of the power beyond that has given it its meaning in the first place. Yet these directors fully comprehend the meaning of their position and the necessity of preserving it! Thus, while they erase their own identity in the face of a higher authority, they become ferocious lions preying on school employees and other subordinates. In a social organization based on pyramidal power structures, the strong prey on the weak.

The Impotent Despot

The function of school administrations can be defined as "despotism by proxy," or a despotism devoid of the necessary authority to manage in a way that effectively regulates school affairs and meets the challenges and problems faced by the school. With this inherent contradiction between appearance and actual power (or lack thereof), school administrations display a dysfunctional or empty formal façade, as most features of schooling are inactive. Though there are training units, production units, and class plans for teaching electronic technology and computer sciences, for the most part they do not function in practice, but only exist as empty forms. Similarly, some schools have Boards of Trustees and Parents' Council, yet they too are often inactive and do not benefit school organization. Directors are helpless to execute routine functions and are unable to maintain order and administer the most basic school affairs.

A clear example of the paradox of the simultaneous power and impotence of school administrations appeared in the school training units and production units. A school director notes the following:

> They told us to make a training unit and a production unit. Both are utterly useless and without any benefit. The training unit is headed by the vice principal for training units and she doesn't know one thing about it! Second, there aren't any resources or facilities available for a production unit. Anyway, what are we supposed to produce? Where is the time for it? Are any class lessons or resources designated for it? No. Is there any space for it inside the school? No. They invent these things to preoccupy us and destroy the educational process even more than it is already.

In fact, the overambitious strategies for reform have the opposite effect. They distort school culture even further by reinforcing the existing status quo. In addition to their inability to implement required programs, school directors face daunting limitations when it comes to dealing effectively with students and parents. One director recounts the story of student violence to illustrate another aspect of the school director's impotence:

> One of my students beat up a teacher, but the real calamity was that the mother came the next day and filed a complaint against the teacher. What should we do with such incidents? We cannot control

those kids. We have no means to control them since hitting is forbidden. Expelling students is also forbidden. So what can I do? In a nearby school a kid in second-grade hit his classmate. The next day the parents of the boy went to the school, beat up the other kid, and beat up the teachers. How can you run such a school?

The director of another school recounts how teachers are vulnerable to parental accusations. He relates how a father fabricated a charge against him after he denied a request to switch the man's daughter from one class section to another:

> One of the parents accused me of hitting his daughter. I swear by God I neither hit the girl nor went near her. The father went to the police station and filed a complaint against me. He then went to the offices of the Undersecretary of the Ministry of Education who conducted an inquiry. The administration is also conducting an inquiry. I am forced to beg the parent for forgiveness [for something I didn't do] so that the father might drop the charges. It has reached such a ridiculous stage.

On top of humiliation and vulnerability, school administrators also suffer from constant suspicions of wrongdoing and a lack of appreciation and respect. In reference to a highly publicized statement by the Minister of Education, that schools have become mafias for private lessons, one director commented, "Have you ever come across a minister who rebukes his own people in public? He distorted our image in front of all the people. He came out and called us a mafia." Another director recounts how the pressure of balancing so many forces took its toll on his colleague's health: "Last year one of our female colleagues suffered a heart attack from the stress, anger, and frustration that comes with working with these kids. And still no one appreciates our suffering."

Nevertheless, it is important to note that school directors tend to trade off surrender for self-interest. There is enough space for them to secure some financial advantages by giving or facilitating private lessons. Directors sometimes allow the school grounds to be used as the place for (illegal) private lessons. They can also exercise their authority and influence their subordinates to their advantage. They are in charge of attendance and absence sheets, holiday schedules, class schedules, and annual reports, and can use this power to negotiate agreements and favors. They can also allow some students to leave school grounds during the school day so that they may attend private lessons outside school. They may also allow leeway and privileges to their favorite teachers. Such a favor might include approving the transfer of a teacher to a more affluent school so that he/she will have more opportunities to give better paying and more numerous private lessons. Thus, directors play a double role inside the school: on the one hand, they preside at the top of the school administration, command obedience, and exercise harsh punishments in order to enforce instructions and regulations; on the other hand, they enforce penal dispensations on a purely personal basis for their own self-interest. Because of this style of administration, social interactions between school members are polarized around enmities, rivalries, and the implicit or explicit conflicts often sugarcoated with hypocrisy and social compliments.

Classroom Culture and the Teacher

Classroom culture refers to those social relations that govern the learning process and influence the formation of the student's character. The teacher, largely responsible for the classroom environment, experiences extreme pressure in the classroom. The despotic hierarchical structure of school relations, together with the socioeconomical conditions of teachers within that hierarchy, lead to a state of alienation; teachers become incapable of controlling their work or managing classrooms and students in a reasonable way.

The relation of teachers to the upper administrative authorities is one of servility and submission. Teachers experience three levels of impotence: social and economic impotence that is a result of their low salary and prevents them from procuring a decent livelihood; creative impotence because they have little autonomy in the classroom and are subject to surveillance and pressure; and an impotence that results from students' full awareness of all of these conditions. Teachers complain bitterly about intrusions by inspectors who try to regulate their work through nitpicking on details such as the way they write the date on the blackboard, the way they mark student notebooks, or the way in which they organize the lesson preparation log. Students witness teachers' daily humiliations at the hands of directors, headmasters, vice principals, inspectors, monitors, supervisors, and coordinators, and can sense their fear when faced with classroom visitors. Moreover, students recognize their own power over their teachers. They sometimes threaten to complain about them and also recognize their teachers' financial impotence and their dire need to give them private lessons.

Teachers repeatedly cite their poor financial condition as the most significant impediment to improving classroom performance. One teacher relates how after twenty-two years of working, his monthly salary was a mere LE 330; he remained a teacher simply because of a lack of alternatives. Low salaries force teachers to either give private lessons or take on a second job of low status, such as driving a taxi or working as a painter. Teachers often note that the classroom had lost much of its meaning because so many students depend on private lessons, rather than the classroom, to learn. Teachers imitate school directors and other figures of authority insofar as they trade surrender, compliance, and submission, for personal interest through the privatization of work. By pursuing the objective of giving private lessons (a practice that allows them to secure a livelihood), teachers sacrifice their mission as educators. Instead of acting as independent, critical, and freethinking individuals who could oppose the effects of the culture of despotism, teachers perpetuate the culture of authoritarianism and despotism.

In principle, teachers operate within rules set by an authoritarian system. They perpetuate a pedagogy based on repetition, memorization, and the elimination of inquiry and questioning (Sharabi 1999, 52). The inflexible static curricula, rigid examination practices, heavily bureaucratic school administration, and constant inspections, all reflect the authoritarianism of school governance. Despite this seeming airtight system, teachers manage to realize their private goals by successfully pursuing the enterprise of private lessons. Thus, teachers are able to accomplish a double role in the social organization of education: they support social authoritarian trends while looking after their personal interests. In this way, teachers resolve the harsh reality of financial impotence.

Even though teachers define teaching in varying terms, they all come down to the basic meaning of teaching as "a pedagogical enterprise that aims at transmitting the maximum amount of information to students." It is no wonder, then, that teachers in all ten schools employ excessive wordiness in their explanations, summaries, and clarifications of curricular material. The hard sciences (including chemistry, biology, physics, computer science, and technology), and the social sciences and humanities, are taught in a style of verbose rhetorical lecturing. Nonacademic subjects such as physical education are neglected, and in all the sample schools there was not a single teacher of music. A student wisely explains the situation:

Education here in Egypt is limited to the sciences and there's no attention paid to the arts, culture, and sports. We actually have a place for sports and a room for musical instruments, calculators, and a computer, but students are not allowed to use any of these because these things cost the government an arm and a leg. This isn't the way to produce an educated Egyptian generation that will advance the country.

What actually takes place inside the classroom is a mirror reflection of the dominant, despotic nature of the social organization of education and society. The classroom pyramid, where the teacher occupies the highest point and students inhabit the bottom, is the smallest and last pyramid within the total framework of the social organization of Egyptian education. Just as directors represent the axis of school organization, teachers represent the axis of classroom organization and the learning process rotates around them. The values that dominate classroom culture—authoritarianism, dominance, control, suppression and submission—permeate school social organization, and society as a whole.

Social Control of Students

A student's time in school is almost entirely devoted to inculcation, memorization, and recitation—with little regard to anything else. Given the values, methods, and means used in teaching and running classes, students are little encouraged to participate in their lessons. On the contrary, instead of playing roles as active participants in the learning process, students are overburdened with unrealistic workloads that thwart their capacities to discuss and debate issues. Furthermore, prevailing teaching methods prevent students from developing essential tools to improve their intelligence, levels of understanding, and ability to acquire the scientific principles to carry out research and critical inquiry. Instead, students are preoccupied with superficial goals of memorizing texts and attaining high grades in examinations. As one teacher explains, "Today's school kids are 'fast food' students! They want the piece of information ready-made and quick. They lack the strong will that would allow them to mold their mind with knowledge and culture." These short-term targets, often empty of real meaning, distract students from trying to understand themselves, from reflecting on issues that are of significance, or from developing an understanding of their social conditions.

Students learn to accept their teachers' absolute authority and control over all aspects of their learning without question. Teachers do not allow students free rein for independent thinking, speech, or movement. Students may answer a question only when a teacher gives permission, and only after they have fulfilled the obsequious rites of submission, obedience, and respect. When a visitor enters a classroom, the teacher orders all students to stand up and they can only sit down in obedience to another command. Many teachers take a cane (*asayya*) with them to the class, conveying a clear message that the cane will be used to enforce the teacher's authority and to met out punishment to those who rebel.

The main problem with schooling from the student's perspective is that they learn to fear and even hate their teachers. Many teachers commonly beat and humiliate their students, to the extent that such behaviors, in some instances, have become staple features of Egyptian public schools. A female student relates her despair at school:

> Relations at school are shitty and disgusting. There is no fun at school. There's nothing but beating and cursing. They don't only beat us on the hands, but on our bodies. They constantly scold and shout at us. If a teacher walks into the classroom and finds us laughing, she will tell us, 'you are losers and you will remain so all of your lives!' None of them believes how torn we are on the inside. We just laugh to hide the pain to be able to go on with our lives.

Another female student bitterly complains about the harsh treatment she receives in school:

> My presence here all day means constant beating and cursing. . . . They even curse our parents. They compare us to animals and they beat us as if we're dumb animals. Isn't that unfair?

Along similar lines, another female student complains:

> They hit us on our bodies, on our backs, on our cheeks. And the foul language they insult us with, calling us 'you daughter of a dog,' you scum[shoe],' 'you slut,' 'you are a worthless piece of garbage,' 'your parents couldn't raise you well,' and many other insults that I can't even say. The reason why we don't like them and why we don't listen to them is because they hate us! They say the teacher is like a father. That is rubbish! Total rubbish!

Even outside the classroom teachers sometimes refer to students in derogatory, humiliating language, as evidenced by the speech of a teacher during a morning assembly when he scolded students for their rowdy behavior and tardiness:

> Third grade, you are garbage. You think of yourselves as men? You're just kids, and not even that. If you don't intend to work and be respectful during the lesson hour then don't even enter through the school gates.... I don't want to see any of you dogs leave the classroom for any reason whatsoever.... Do I make myself clear?

Beating, ridiculing, degrading, and belittling students are all means of enforcing the hegemony of the master slave principle in the classroom. Obedience in this case comes about as the result of fear rather than love or respect. The result is the formation of students who feel deprived of self-confidence and self-respect as well as respect for others. Understandably, this prevailing culture that includes violence, aggression, cruelty, corporal punishment, and humiliation, finally drives students to fear and hate both teacher and school. A dejected student relates how she transferred dislike of her teacher to dislike of her schoolwork. After explaining how a male teacher beats her "like an animal" she adds: "Why should I like the class [subject] of a teacher who I don't like in the first place? When I open the textbook of the class he's teaching I see his face looking at me... I simply close the book."

Instead of liberating minds, education serves as a form of inculcation which asks students to replicate the teacher's message (Darrag 1992, 16). Teachers, then, enchain students with instructions, commands, and prohibitions. Thus, the role of teachers is inversed; they preclude students from true curiosity by promoting a kind of learning that is confined to memorization and duplication. The Arab sociologist Hisham Sharabi refers to this process whereby the student's critical facilities are thwarted as "educational terrorism" (1999). Indeed, we find that students learn to not only memorize pieces of information, but also learn the principles of submission: giving-in to authority; obedience to the teacher; and uncritical acceptance of school texts. Alternatively, they learn to hate learning itself. Within this framework, the possibility of free discussion or knowledge production simply disappears. Students are not only ignorant but also incapable of independent thought or reasoning.

Socioeconomic Discrimination

Public schools discriminate in many ways against students of low socioeconomic backgrounds. This type of discrimination is most apparent when students are required to pay for participation in certain activities such as extracurricular sports programs or school trips. Even though the required sums may be paltry (no more than a few cents), the inability of some students to pay deprives them of joining in. Students without the means are also unable to take part in summer skills-training courses such as how to use an advanced calculator. Those who can afford the courses achieve higher grades in accounting while the poor make do with rudimentary theoretical instruction given during regular school lessons. A lack of means can also contribute to harsher punishments. Some schools impose a small fine on students as a punishment for arriving late to school. Those who carry money on them are able to pay the fine and head to their classrooms. Those unable to pay remain standing by the school gates feeling utterly humiliated and put-down.

School uniforms represent another mark of inequality and suffering of the poorer students. Teachers and directors often humiliate and sometimes even hit or dismiss girls who cannot afford proper uniform attire. A girl from one school explains her problem:

> I only have colored headscarves and cannot afford to buy a white headscarf like they want me to. Sometimes they kick me out of school. How can I handle the humiliation? What can I do? I'm sick of my kind of life, just sick of it all!

Teachers seem to lack empathy with poor and destitute students and may even despise them. Despite the modest social background of many teachers, they often adopt a stance of the powerful toward the weak, look upon poorer children with disdain, and distance themselves from them. They discriminate against them and offer their educational services preferentially. The more flagrant expressions of discrimination appear mainly in the context of school-sponsored private lessons that only richer students can afford to attend. The poorest children are unable to pay for these lessons. Students who do not take any form of private lessons complain of being picked on and insulted in class, beaten disproportionately to the others, or simply utterly neglected. A student explains the inequitable situation:

> When a girl takes lessons with one of the teachers she passes [the exam] by some kind of divine intervention even though she might be a lazy bum, while a hard-working girl fails. Sometimes during an exam the proctor recognizes the daughter of a teacher so he asks her, 'do you need anything?' As for the penniless girl, well, no one knows who she is.

A student who cannot pay for a study group or private lessons is unlikely to compete successfully, continue onto higher education, and achieve social recognition. In essence, the poor are deprived of equal learning opportunities and educational equity, all of which make their possibilities for social mobility highly difficult if not nearly impossible. Students are fully aware that the school system is not a fair meritocracy and that it favors those of a higher social level. Students fully comprehend the contradictions about education promoting civic values and social equity. Thus, students develop deep resentment and disrespect for their teachers and transfer their negative feelings to the school.

A Pathology of Cheating

The schooling process fosters the pursuit of selfish ends without regard for public welfare. If we establish that the political culture of the school is based on a pyramidal system in which subservience (by way of false humility), hypocrisy, and forsaking hard work are the norms, then it follows that cheating will emerge as an overriding characteristic of the system. Directors and teachers, both of whom organize much of their work around securing private lessons, often attend to their personal interests above other responsibilities. Students are single-mindedly preoccupied with their grades and personal success at the cost of collegiality, cooperation with their classmates, and community building. One teacher describes the student-student relationship as follows: "I have observed that students' relationships are based on enmity and selfishness. During each lesson, I have to listen to at least three students complain about each other." In such a situation, all members of the school community are susceptible to pursuing their individual interests at any cost, including the violation of not only school rules and regulations, but also the ethical values of society at large.

Cheating, a means of obtaining privileges without deserving them, represents a detrimental side effect of the authoritarian teacher-student relationship which, in effect, reflects corrupt social relations at the macro level. Society itself suffers from a political culture of despotism whereby economic and political power belong to a miniscule minority. The despotic powers treat the masses as tools and pieces to be played and moved at will. Despotism, in other words, starts with an act of inversion whereby it falsely represents its governing processes as democratic, a claim which in and of itself cheats the public. Cheating then spreads rapidly within the successive pyramidal structures. Tragically, cheating comes to be supported by members of the general public as a means to achieve their own everyday pursuits. Members of the public may even believe that they are cheating the system—and thereby subverting power—when they conduct their private businesses through cheating. In such a way, the pursuit of individual means and ends through cheating become entirely normalized.

The fact that the education system is exam-driven contributes to an even higher prevalence of cheating. Not only might students cheat on exams to improve their scores, but school administrators and teachers, under pressure to pass students along from one grade to the next and avoid penalties that sometimes fall on poor-performing schools, may help students to pass exams. One director recounts how some teachers actually write out exam answers on the blackboard so their functionally illiterate students might pass their elementary school certificates. As a result, many students begin the next stage of preparatory schooling without knowing how to read and write. Aside from leaving primary school as functional illiterates, another unfortunate consequence of this practice is that students learn that cheating is acceptable.

The real tragedy rests in the fact that cheating is not only limited to examinations, but extends to all aspects of the educational process. Why should a student care to study or learn anything if success will be determined through cheating? Why should teachers exert themselves to honestly teach lessons when all that they do—or not do—amounts to nothing? Inevitably, private lessons, together with cheating, corrupt the school system and erode ethical values essential to the development and advancement of a civil society: work, the drive for achievement, and a desire to achieve excellence. The continuous indoctrination of generations of students to the habits of cheating is reproduced, together with the cheater character which becomes deeply embedded in the culture. Cheating flourishes in Egyptian society to such an extent that it becomes acceptable, condoned, and justified.

Student Resistance and Counter Violence

Students from low-income schools confront coercion, frustration, and intellectual, physical, and emotional abuse on a daily basis. They are also subject to a curriculum that is often criticized as sterile, ineffectual, and useless to the practical needs of these students. As one student points out, "We need a curriculum that benefits us in our practical lives. Our current curriculum is useless!" Students also despair because of uncertain employment futures. A teacher explains:

> There is one question that students, both male and female, ask repeatedly: 'What comes after I finish with education? What will happen?' The young cannot find any employment after graduation and students have lost all incentives in the educational system.

Perhaps most dangerous of all, some students, by going through the system, appear to lose their self-confidence, lose their trust in others, and learn to hate themselves. Still others choose the path of resistance and rebellion.

Students, especially the ones from low-income areas, appear to be increasingly slipping out of the grip of adult authority. They show their rejection of teacher authority and oppression through a refusal to cooperate to the normal routines. During class time they might sleep, doodle, chat, mock the teacher's lecturing, fake fights with their classmates, or interrupt the teacher. They may try to embarrass teachers by asking difficult and strange questions, raise issues that are disruptive and distracting, joke and make pleasantries, or sing and beat their desks like drums and make strange sounds. They may even jump out of a classroom window or jump over the classroom chairs. Often they will not bring their stationary and school supplies to class and will not do their homework. A student may attempt to obstruct teaching activities, may disrespectfully talk back to a teacher, and may taunt a teacher by saying, "You can't beat me. Hitting is forbidden." Sometimes a student, either male or female, may snatch the cane out of a teacher's hand to prevent a beating, or may complain to the school administration or district administration, or even to the police, that a teacher has breached the law in beating them.

Some students simply refuse to participate in school and express this through repeated absences. Skipping classes or whole days of school constitutes a form of escape from the repression and intellectual persecution that surrounds them. Indeed, escaping school represents both a rejection of the oppressive school culture and an assertion of a right to freedom. Thus, truancy can be read as an attempt by students to liberate themselves from the traditions and customs of the school and family. It is a means to express their maturity (whether manliness or femininity). Their escape is often involved with going out in mixed groups of girls or boys, smoking, and sometimes taking drugs.

Some students also develop a sense of almost gang-like solidarity to resist classroom culture and bypass school rules. Despite internal rifts and the development of individual interests (as noted above), students often band together against "the enemy." One director describes this tactic as "a gang feeling amongst the students." This form of solidarity has the effect of students encouraging each other to resist unfair practices against them. Students will often cover-up for their colleagues, even when doing so leads to group punishment. They prefer group punishment and solidarity over betraying a colleague.

Some students, however, express their frustration and anger by more violent and aggressive means. Many school directors report a marked rise in acts of student vandalism. The director of a boys' school comments: "Students just lie in waiting for the opportunity to steal any school property... desk drawers, chairs, whatever.... They break doors and windows. Kids steal the windows' aluminum frames.... We call the parents but they never come...." These methods, though negative, reflect a determination to reject and object to what is taking place inside schools and classrooms, and a desire to change them.

Arguably, the most dangerous student response to school despotism and suppression is counterviolence, a new alarming phenomenon that does not seem to have a precedent in Egyptian history. A school director notes with resignation, "Students just wait for the opportunity to commit acts of violence against the teacher, himself, or the school." This new wave of violence is a loud and clear warning for both those who abuse and those who are abused.

For the violence will not stop at damaging school property, beating teachers, and interstudent fighting. It has already reached graver levels. The director of a boys' school points to this danger:

> Around 90 percent of students come to school equipped with soft weapons (blades and knives). They have extremely aggressive tendencies and are very much affected by what's happening outside in the streets. We have a daily average caseload of about three to four students who are taken to the medical center to get some stitches or other treatment for their injuries from attacks.

A male student described the aggressive and violent youth culture of which he is a part:

There is hardly any respect at school. The acceptable language here is, 'if you have a weapon you win.' Even when kids greet each other it's mostly in curses, swearing, and naming parents and family in foul language. Anger and fighting, stabbing with knives and blades, are all very common here. There's even a boy who smokes in class and offers us [cigarettes]. All of this is of course bad.

Boys' anger and violence can turn against teachers, school directors, and even the school itself. Boys often express aggression and prove their manliness by challenging the authority of the teacher. A student explains,

Each one of these kids wants to show the others that he's a man...and brave...that he isn't afraid of anyone...not even the teachers. Sometimes the teacher approaches them with a cane to hit them...they catch hold of the cane and snatch it from his hands... Sometimes they may even throw it in his face.

Anther director speaks about the rise of student violence:

These kids have aggressive destructive tendencies. . . . They physically assault teachers. Come and see for yourself during the evening shift. Watch how teachers look when they are leaving the school. . . . Students are lying in waiting for them with pocketknives. They beat up teachers. Once a student threw a stone at my head and wounded me.

Another teacher still had scars on his face from when students threw pieces of wood at him from the window.

The girls use slightly different tactics. While they might not hit back teachers and vandalize property, they try to shame their teachers publicly, or threaten to report them to the policy or other authorities. A girl rudely asked her teacher, "Why are you staring at me this way?" Another girl screamed at the teacher when he tried to hit her: "You can't hit me!" thereby shaming him in front of the other students and threatening him with recourse.

Clearly, students in these poor schools are desperately attempting to break away from the hold of class culture hegemony, violate its rules, and resist by any possible means, even by assaulting school staff or stealing and vandalizing school property. As one boy explains:

Everything these students do is perfectly natural. . . . What could you expect from a kid who was hit by the teacher, kicked around, hit in the face and on the back of his neck [the spot of dignity]? These are absolutely normal behaviors!

Students are displaying an extremely aggressive and confrontational stance towards the school system in a way unparalleled in the history of Egyptian education.

Conclusion: The Production and Reproduction of Culture in Egyptian Schools

The public-sector school represents a microcosm of the authoritarian state. In essence, all state apparatuses and institutions replicate the schools in that they attempt to teach, form, and indoctrinate social consciousness in the principles of submission and control, the permissible and the forbidden (Darraj 1992, 15). The despotism inside schools, as in the larger society, is based on a monopoly of decision-making processes, relationships of dominance and submission, and the negation of difference or alternate points of view. Schools clearly reproduce a despotic personality.

Despite government rhetoric about school reform towards more democracy and participation, the very organizational structure of schools hampers participation in decision-making at all levels. Each member of the school community performs the dual role of suppressor and suppressed. The school director acts, in effect, as an agent of despotism executing his/her despotic power in proxy of a higher authority. Yet, at the same time, she/he is fearful of higher authority and is incapable of practicing true management and solving everyday school problems. When a school director undertakes actions such as facilitating private lessons, she/he trades off her/his submission for a private interest. Teachers, burdened by dire financial circumstances and despairing a lack of autonomy in the classroom, also pursue private interests. When they use their position and power to secure private lessons from their students, teachers accelerate the moral degeneration of education and forsake the essential mission of education and pedagogy.

The classroom, reflecting the inequality and oppression of the larger society, becomes a place where students, especially the poor, are blocked from any real learning opportunities and suffer constant moral, physical, and psychological abuse. Teachers maintain order and discipline through the relentless use of physical violence and insults that not only degrade the student, but inhibit his/her emotional and mental development. In such a way, classroom culture promotes, or reproduces, the despotic personality which is characterized by values of passivity, servility, fear, resentment, impotence, lying, and cheating.

The dismal conditions at schools have led many students to either dropout or not attend classes regularly. Through desertion, the student silently expresses his/her rejection of school, hatred of what it represents, and a mutiny against it. Although dropping out of school will likely lead to continued marginalization, it may also represent a way for the student to escape the process of *reproduction* inherent in the school experience and lead to a potentially self-empowered *production*. The nineteenth-century Egyptian activist, 'Abd ar-Rahman al-Kawakibi, famously said:

> Who is more worthy than the one who is held captive in one land, to
> turn to another where he can find his freedom; [certainly] a free dog
> has a better life than that of a captive lion. (2002, 28)

For those students who opt to attend school, they increasingly mock the values that govern the school world as a way of claiming their rights and trying to change it. Students seem to be increasingly refusing to accept insults, ridicule, humiliation, and physical violence, and rebel by confronting violence with counterviolence. By many accounts, students are increasingly involved in threatening behaviors and beating teachers and administrators, fighting violently between themselves (sometimes with weapons), and vandalizing school property.

Students also attempt to obtain their rights through the power of the law. They are becoming bold and savy enough to file complaints against abusive teachers and school administrators with the police. Going to the police station is a definite form of aggression aimed at the school as well as an attempt to slander it and expose it to the outside world. Students may pay a heavy price for their attempts at resisting and standing up to the teachers' abusive behavior. The matter often ends with students dropping out of school or failing in their studies, but some seem nevertheless willing to take the risk. All of these innovative cultural forms, including recourse to the police, constitute attempts to break away from corrupt rules and traditions of the classroom culture of despotism.

Public schools serving the lower income and poverty-stricken classes appear to be witnessing a state of anarchy manifest at all levels of the educational and learning process. Students and their parents in actuality, are influencing the course of affairs in these schools. The cultural reproduction instigated by students themselves, whatever its forms of expression, shows clearly that poor students reject the vision of the school towards them and the meaning of education as upheld by their teachers. They attempt to influence and change school conditions and to push teachers and administrators to redefine their relations and to alter their behavior with students. These changes, however, tend to be temporary as they simply absorb the excessive anger of students. The problem of the despotic social organization remains at heart the same.

For the most part, students' attempts to change their social universe do not serve their long-term interests. Because social mobility remains so tied to academic success, their rejection of the school system may lead to their foregoing opportunities for social mobility and a perpetuation of the cycle of reproduction. The question then, that needs to be asked, is: Can the poor realize liberation within the context of the current conditions of public schools? Egyptian public schools for the poor loudly proclaim a culture of despotism, but their students speak another message, a message of a culture of freedom. Any discussion on classroom culture in Egyptian schools must finally include a discourse on both despotism and liberty. A new formation of education—of school and classroom relations—where liberty constitutes an essential component, can only come about from a clear understating of the current reality.

Notes to Chapter 2

1. I refer most especially to the works by the following proponents of critical education theories who are concerned with concepts such as "social reproduction," "cultural production," "resistance," "the educated person," and "the formation of cultural identity": (Apple 1979, 1982; Giroux 1983, 1992; Gilroy, 1987; Levinson and Holland 1996; Levinson et al 2000; Torres and Mitchell 1998).

2. I would like to express my gratitude to Linda Herrera, the coordinator of "The Culture and Education in Egypt Working Group." She revised and supported the thesis of this study from the very start and supplied me with valuable criticism, which has helped in the development of the study and its completion. She had made available most of the references and literature needed for this research and helped me in getting research funds from the Population Council, West Asia and North Africa, to carry out this study. My gratitude naturally extends to the executives of the Population Council.

3. It is noteworthy that in 1982, "The Society of the Sociology of Education" was established in the League of Modern Education in Egypt. The

proponents of this movement, including the author, advocated the study of social relations inside schools and classrooms from the framework of Critical Pedagogy. Unfortunately, the Society did not fully realize its call and did not transform it into any practical action (see Naguib 1988; Center of Political and Strategic Studies 1986, 15).

4. Among the pioneering studies in Egyptian education are Hamid Ammar's *Growing up in an Egyptian village: Silwa, Province of Aswan* (1954), in which the author describes the social organization of the local rural society, and analyzes issues of social and cultural change in the village of Silwa. We should also point out the valuable work of Safaa Abd al-Aziz (1981) on the hidden curriculum.

5. Our main reference for analyzing the phenomenon of despotism in school and classroom culture is Faysal Darraj's prominent study, "*Despotism of Culture and Culture of Despotism*" (1992). We also benefited from the thoughtful and realistic insights posed by Hisham Sharabi (1999) on the relation of school culture and classroom culture. The author depends extensively on both these sources for definitions and formulations used in the present study.

References

Abd al-Aziz, Safaa. 1981. Teachers' perception of grading: A sociological study of the hidden curriculum. MA thesis, University of Pittsburg.

Ahmad, 'Abd al-Sami Sayyid. 1999. The usefulness of the theory of coercion in the sociology of education. *Contemporary Education*, no. 16 (Dec.):43–94. [in Arabic].

Al-Ahram Center of Political and Strategic Studies. 1986. Conference Proceedings of the League of Modern Education, 2–5 April, 1984. Cairo: Dar al-Fikr al-Mu'asir.

Al-Bialawi, Hassan. 1986. Al-Tarbeyya wa Baniya al-Tafawat al-Ijtimaiyya al-Tabaqy: Dirasat Naqdeyya fi fikr Pierre Bourdieu. [Education and Structures of Social Class Inequities: Critical Analysis of Pierre Bourdieu.] *Dirasat Tarbaweyya* [Pedagogical Studies], 3 (June): 119–169.

———. 1993. *Fi `Ilm Ijtima` Al-Tarbaweyya* [In the Science of Sociology of Education.] Cairo: 'Alam al-Kitab.

Al-Kawakibi, Abd al-Rahman. 2002. *Taba`ia al-Istibdad wa Musar`a al-Ist`ibad* [The Nature of Despotism and the Struggle of the Enslaved.] Damascus: Dar al-Mada.

Ammar, Hamed. 1954. *Growing up in an Egyptian village: Silwa, Province of Aswan*. London: Routledge and Kegan Paul.

Apple, Michael. 1979. *Ideology and curriculum*. London: Routledge and Kegan Paul.

———. 1982. *Cultural and economic reproduction in American education: Essays in class, ideology and the state*. Boston: Routledge and Kegan Paul.

Darraj, Faysal. 1992. Istibdad al-Thaqafa wa Thaqafat al-Istibdad [Despotism of Culture and Culture of Despotism.] *Fusul* 11:2 (summer): 9–23. [in Arabic].

Gilroy, Paul. 1987. *"Ain't No Black in the Union Jack": The Cultural Politics of Race and Nation*. London: Hutchinson.

Giroux, Henry. 1983. *Theory and Resistance in Education: A Pedagogy of the Opposition*. London: Heinemann Educational Books.

———. 1992. *Border crossings: Cultural workers and the politics of education*. New York: Routledge.

Levinson, Bradley, Douglas Foley, and Dorothy Holland. 1996. The Cultural Production of the Educated Person: An Introduction. In *The Cultural Production of the Educated Person: Critical Ethnographies of Schooling and Local Practice*, ed. B. A. Levinson et al., 1–54. New York: State University of New York Press.

———. et al., eds. 2000. *Schooling the Symbolic Animal: Social and Cultural Dimensions of Education*. New York: Rowman and Littlefield.

Naguib, Kamal. 1986. Al-Democratiyya wa al-Manhaj: Dirasat al-Itijahat al-Tarbaweyya al-Muasir. [Democracy and Methodology: A Study of Contemporary Trends in Education.] In *Democracy and Education in Egypt*, 52–71. Cairo: Contemporary Education Publications.

———. 1988. Al-Fikr al-Siyasi wa al-Tarbawy lil Mualim al-Masry [Political and Pedagogical Thought of the Egyptian Educator.] *Contemporary Education*, 10 (June): 55–130.

Sharabi, Hisham. 1999. *Muqadimaat lil Dirasat al-Mujtama` al-Araby* [Introductions to the Study of Arab Society.] 6th edition. Beirut: Dar Nelson.

Torres, Carlos Alberto and Theodore Mitchell. 1998. *Sociology of education: Emerging perspectives*. Albany: State University of New York Press.

Willis, Paul. 1981. *Learning to labor: How working class kids get working class jobs*. New York: Columbia University Press.

3

Subsistence Education: Schooling in a Context of Urban Poverty

AHMED YOUSSOF SAAD

Summary

Members of the poor and oppressed classes often view education as their last line of defense in the face of social marginalization. Despite the fact that education at all levels is pyramidal in nature and tends to reproduce social stratification, it still provides the poor with hope for opportunities and social mobility. In reality, though, parents learn to expect only the bare minimum from the education system, to expect a "subsistence education." Why is there such a disparity between the rhetoric and the reality? How do the poor and oppressed read their world? How do their schools attempt to impose on them a particular reading of the world? This chapter, based on a critical ethnographic study of a double-shift public preparatory school in a low-income neighborhood in Cairo, will attempt to answer these questions. Observations in the field revealed that teachers and pupils perceive their reality through two contrasting texts simultaneously: on the one hand there is the official reality as it is presented and depicted in formal texts, and on the other hand there is the impoverished reality in the grip of which they find themselves and which they are ashamed to admit.

Reading the "Word" and Reading the "World" of Egyptian Education

In his *Teachers as Cultural Workers: Letters to Those Who Dare Teach*, and especially in the letter entitled, "Reading the World/Reading the

Word," Paulo Freire puts forward the concepts of "reading the world of reality," and "reading the word of the text" (1998, 17–26). The former refers to how one learns to read and better perceive his/her own life and lived experiences, whereas the latter refers to the reading of an already lived reality. This critical ethnographic study of a double-shift public preparatory school in a low-income neighborhood in Cairo is an attempt to understand the dialectic between how the poor read their world and how their schools attempt to impose upon them a particular reading of the "word." It is similarly an attempt by the author to engage in a critical reading of his own society. For the act of reading, as Freire so eloquently states, means that "we take critical ownership of the formation of our selves, which socially and gradually, over time, become active and conscious, speaking, reading, and writing, and which are both inherently and socially constructed." (24). Freire reminds us that reading is a taxing intellectual process, one that asks much of us by way of "comprehension and communication" (19). Those who do not read critically, it can be argued, do not genuinely learn, do not fully read.

To tackle the role of the school in contemporary society requires a layered understanding of the institution. The school functions according to a set of laws that belong to a local society, a region, and a world. This means that the culture of this institution is shaped through a series of concentric circles, influenced by multiple factors, pressures, conflicts of interest, opposing intentions regarding its existence, as well as the conflict between historic and transient elements. The individual's interaction with the school ranges from total obedience to total resistance; for just as the institution has a culture and a history, so too the individual. Within the school, in other words, we can find a range of behaviors that can be interpreted as supporting theories from "reproduction" to "resistance."[1]

The Arab region struggles with difficult social, political, and economic realities. As documented most recently in the UNDP *Arab Human Development Reports*, the more serious challenges facing the region are high illiteracy rates, the deterioration of the quality of education, the slow pace of scientific research and technological development, the weakness of the production base and an inability to compete, the spread of poverty and rapidly increasing unemployment rates, limitations of human liberties, and the lack of empowerment for women (UNDP, 2002 and 2003). These social problems are compounded by political challenges facing the region, especially after September 11, 2001 and include: an exacerbation of Israeli military provocation in Palestine; a decline in Arab governments of justice, freedom, and human rights; increased regional military conflict; the lagging of the Arab region compared to other Third World regions in terms of political participation and democracy; the presence of governing structures with a powerful executive branch controlling all state apparatuses without transparency or accountability; and the general absence of freedoms of expression and organization. These challenges and dangers, aggravated by the pervasive, all-encompassing effects of globalization, are reaching alarming proportions in the Arab world.

Since Egypt's Open Door Policy of 1974, governmental political and economic policies have favored the forceful return of capitalism and integration into global markets at all levels of society. This reversal of its prior socialist policies is the reality in which Egypt finds itself. Being the world's oldest surviving centralized state does not much help Egypt. Its social structure shares many features with other Third World countries whose economies had been absorbed into the capitalist world market in the colonial and postcolonial eras. Just as economic liberalization has marginalized the oppressed social classes, education might, in the shadow of privatization policies, marginalize the sons and daughters of the same classes. With the rise of privatization of schooling, formal education has contributed to ever-widening social inequality. Just as the ship of the nation can no longer embrace everyone in the light of the economy's globalization, so too the ship of education. The slogan, "Education for All," which was adopted by world governments in Jomtien in 1990, thus comes to mean equality of opportunity in climbing aboard the ship of education without necessarily implying the ability to stay onboard or to save one's place till the end of the voyage. Just as there are sharp differences between private schools and public schools to the advantage of the former, there are also sharp differences between one private school and the next. Within public schools there also exist striking disparities based on factors such as location and the socioeconomic level of its users. Public schools in low-income neighborhoods have suffered the worst forms of deterioration.

Defining "Class" in an Urban Poor Neighborhood

The school under study is located in an urban area of Cairo that dates to the 1980s and consists of government subsidized housing complexes

and informal slum housing. The area was initially built to house relo-
cated populations, such as those who were moved out of slums in the
city center after their homes were demolished by governmental decrees
on the grounds that the capital needed a face-lift and also needed to
alleviate congestion. The area's population consists of a minority of
government employees and a majority of craftsmen, wandering peddlers, the unemployed, recent rural immigrants seeking employment
opportunities in the city, and some newly-wed professionals seeking
affordable housing. With minor exceptions due to individual initiative,
the area is characterized by a seemingly chaotic or haphazard use of
space and is enveloped with an air of poverty, disharmony, and a lack
of cleanliness and order. Piles of garbage appear throughout the streets
and a gloomy mud-colored dust covers the buildings. In the unpaved
side streets, the dust more often than not mixes with open sewage, a
sign that the area has provided refuge to more inhabitants than the
number for which it was designed. It also indicates the neglect of this
area by the local municipality.

The overpopulated area houses a medley of inhabitants from a variety of socio-economic and educational backgrounds. It can be said that
in Egyptian society, similar to many Third World societies, it is generally
difficult to map out the class structure or to clearly demarcate where one
class ends and another begins (Al-Issawi 1989, 32–40). Nevertheless, and
at the risk of oversimplifying a much more complex reality, three general
social classes may be identified. At the highest pole is an upper class
composed of big land owners, business elite, and the state or bureaucratic bourgeoisie. At the lower pole resides the lower class, the poor
majority that includes poor peasants, agricultural and nonagricultural
laborers, petty craftsmen and petty merchants, the urban poor who work
in the informal sector, and the unemployed. Between these two poles of
extreme wealth and near abject poverty, is an undefined, stagnant middle
class without straightforward distinguishing features (Ouda 1995,
26–28). The inhabitants of the area under study can be described as
belonging to the lower and middle classes.

The public housing units by and large contain single family apartments consisting of one bedroom, a reception area, a kitchen, and a
bathroom. Each building in the housing complex contains twenty apartments, four on each of the five floors, and each apartment houses a
family of, on average, five persons. Apartments located on the top floors
tend to expand vertically through the ceiling and onto the roof to

accommodate the unforeseen growth of families. Ground floor apartments, as a result of the demand for more space and also for financial gain that comes from opening street-front businesses, spill out onto the public space. The front rooms of these apartments may serve as cobweb-ridden workshops with walls covered in oil and grease stains, shops selling cheap soap, tea, no-brand detergents in plastic bags, children's sweets, imported soft drinks, and American cigarettes, cultivated plots of land fenced in by bits and pieces of dismantled wooden boxes, tin sheets and wire, coffee shops at which tea, coffee, and water pipes may be smoked, not to mention illegal substances such as hashish. Late at night certain coffee shops become sites where local male youth congregate to watch videos or films shown on satellite TV, films that are sometimes pornographic in nature. Some of the local unemployed male youth may opt, in the no-man's-land of the public space that is the street, to get together to play a sport that does not require much space, to play ping pong or billiards (which in older times was the prerogative of the aristocracy), or, to bring a television set outdoors to play video games.

Forms of entertainment for children are limited to games that may be played in the street: football, thieves and robbers, or pranks directed against each other or those living on the ground floor. The children, mostly barefoot and wearing tatty clothes, throw stones at cats and dogs, or chase the ducks, geese, and chickens bred by the residents of rural origins. The children of professional parents rarely play in the street due to their parents' dread of them mixing with the children of the backward (*mutakhalaf*) social groups. These parents prefer to involve their children in the cultural activities offered by the local library or by the children's club named after Egypt's first lady, which provides entertainment, books, and cultural services. The low-income children and youth for whom these clubs are intended, more often than not, decline to make use of them.

The majority of women in the area do not work outside the home owing to a lack of skills and education, a lack of opportunity, or the conviction—based on tradition or religion—that a woman's place is in the home. When they do have paid jobs, the noneducated women work in low-skill jobs such as maids, manual laborers in low or no-tech factories, or as shop assistants. There is a high degree of school dropouts among the daughters of nonprofessionals, or, at best, they complete the preparatory level of education (grade 8). The daughters of professional mothers, on the other hand, tend to remain in school and have aspirations for the university.

In the late 1980s and early 1990s, the area was known as a conservative Islamist stronghold, and one of its mosques was raided by police
more than once. Still today. signs of Islamist conservatism remain: the
overwhelming majority of the women in the area, regardless of class and
education, observe a Muslim dress code, and most of the men sport
beards (a sign of religious piety or, sometimes, extremism). Many slogans
with an Islamic content, such as "The veil is chastity and purity," "Islam
is the solution," and "He who does not pray is an infidel" are written on
the walls in the area. Some grocers hang a photocopy of the official Al-
Azhar decree by the Grand Mufti, "Smoking is religiously prohibited" to
advertise the fact that their shop no longer sells cigarettes. When compared to the neighboring coffee shops with hashish and pornography on
offer for young men, the incongruity of this area is apparent.

The community members of this disjointed, contradictory, and
mixed environment defy easy categorization. Among the least fortunate
of the residents we find widespread illiteracy, a low level of social and
political participation, a tendency to live hand-to-mouth, the widespread
phenomenon of abandoned wives and children, a feeling of fatalism and
surrender, and high dropout rates from school. In this environment, the
personality of the oppressed is formed, bearing all the elements of the
culture of oppression, sensing helplessness and insecurity in the face of
the violence imposed by master, policeman, and landlord who use force,
and by the bureaucrat who can get papers moving or stop them. In the
face of these interlocking forms of oppression, the oppressed have no
option but to suffer a sense of dependency and inferiority, to submit to
being objects rather than equals in all matter of social relations (Hegazy
1986, 36–37).

In relation to the very poor, members of the professional classes
seem relatively well-off, at least insofar as their participation and success
in education is concerned. Parents with means, especially those parents
belonging to professional groups, usually send their children to private
schools in order to escape from "the public school inferno" as some of
them call it, and to keep their children from mixing with the children of
"doorkeepers, craftsmen, wandering peddlers, and thieves." Students
with no other choice enroll in the public schools. How do these children
perceive their world? What is the psychological state of the teachers who
must work in an environment of deprivation and contradictions? What
will the interactions look like?

Inside the School: Methodological Challenges

The school under study is a double-shift public sector preparatory school (grades 6–8). The researcher gained an intimate understanding of the school environment and school culture through conducting sustained ethnographic research on a daily basis over a period of five weeks (from 2/22/2003 to 3/03/2003). Initially, the researcher encountered certain difficulties in the field, part of which were due to his being Egyptian and being familiar with the conditions he was observing. In other words, the researcher's familiarity with the facts, events, actions, and reactions under observation initially dulled his observational capabilities. He was not intellectually stimulated during the first few days of fieldwork, so he began to be proactive, to change his position from passive-observer to participant-observer. He began more actively engaging with the school community in a way that led to more interactive encounters and a greater degree of awareness.

During the first two weeks, the researcher interpreted the facts and events in a largely negative light. He gradually began to see things from the perspective of the actors themselves, something that is fundamental to the ethnographic approach. Yet he was faced with challenges arising from the fact that ethnography is not customary in Egyptian schools. Members of the school community are used to research based on surveys that take only a few hours to conduct, and they were apprehensive of the researcher observing and taking notes on every minute detail of their interactions. The researcher initially felt awkward, and experienced great difficulty in penetrating the silence, or in getting beyond the sugarcoated image that the school members tried to convey. He had to explain to them the nature of his methodology and research and to assure them that his motives were purely academic. Both school principals suspected the researcher of being a disguised member of a follow-up committee, sent by some branch of the Ministry of Education. Despite these initial suspicions, most members of the school community became convinced that the researcher was genuinely an education researcher and felt at ease enough to return to their natural, spontaneous course of behavior.

The ethnographic research techniques used were those of passive-observation, participant-observation, and open-ended interviews (Spindler 1997). Observations took place in a variety of situations and with different school actors and included: interactions of the two principals with teachers, parents, follow-up committees, students, workers, the school doctor, and the rest of the school staff; sustained classroom observations across subjects, grades, and during inspections by MOE supervisors; interactions between teachers and pupils throughout the school day; and student interactions during break times and before and after school. In addition to observations, and to confirm some of the conclusions to which the observations led, extended interviews were conducted with the two principals and some of the supervisors, members of the follow-up committees, students, and teachers of the different subjects.

The School Environment

During the period of research, the school served as a boys' preparatory school during the morning shift from 7:30 a.m. to 12:30 p.m., and as a girls' preparatory school from 1:30 p.m. to 6:30: p.m. The pupils were between the ages of eleven and fourteen years. According to school statistics, the academic performance of the girls surpassed that of the boys, with 47 percent of girls passing the level of eighth grade, and 32 percent of boys passing the same year. There was roughly the same number of teachers in both schools, with sixty-two teachers in the girls' school, and sixty in the boys' school. While both schools had a mix of female and male teachers, the ratios differed, with 20 percent of female teachers in the boys' school versus 80 percent of female teachers in the girls' school. There were roughly eight hundred fifty students per school. With nineteen classrooms in the school, each class had an average of forty-five students.

The school was situated near a street with mainly automobile repair shops and housing complexes similar to the ones described above. The school's outer walls were coated in yellow lime paint and bore, in green, the slogan "My school is beautiful, clean, advanced, and productive" which, according to a Ministry of Education (MOE) decree, all schools must exhibit. The same slogan appeared in red on the school's iron green gates. Crowning the main gate was a yellow sign with the name of the school at the top in black, and, at the bottom, the word "Boys" on the right and "Girls" on the left.

All visitors were requited to check in to an "officer on duty" room which was located to the left of the main gate. The L-shaped four storey main building was situated to the right of the school entrance across a sandy courtyard, at the end of which was a row of short trees, a single palm tree, and some grass. In the middle of this row was a metal flagpole with the Egyptian flag. Broken desks and mere iron skeletons of desks were scattered throughout the courtyard. The first floor contained the rooms of the principal and the school doctor, the library, a room shared by the social worker and several teachers, a compact music room, a lab, some classrooms, the faculty lavatory, and the canteen. The second and third floors consisted entirely of classrooms, with the exception of the room designated for home economics, which was situated on the second floor. The computer lab (a small room) and the remaining classrooms were all on the fourth floor.

The first room on view to the visitor was the principal's room with its set of old, worn armchairs, a threadbare, faded carpet, renovated chairs full of nails that could rip the clothes of the person sitting in them, and two metal desks—one for the principal of each shift. On each desk was a telephone which each principal took special care to put under lock and key in a drawer or a closet at the end of his/her shift. On the walls hung posters with data about each of the schools such as class schedules, statistics about the teachers, and information about the school clubs. The next door was the social worker's room, the largest administrative room, but it was hardly an ideal place for a private conversation since it was also used by some teachers, who, when in the room and seated at old desks placed side by side, would chat, mark pupils' notebooks, or eat and drink.

The music room was the smallest room on the first floor and served more as a storage room than a classroom. It contained some basic instruments such as percussion instruments and a xylophone. The adjoining room was the school library. A special department of the Ministry of Education selects books for all public school libraries. Most of these books are cheaply produced and deal with religion or are known books of Arabic literature. In the middle of the library, across from the librarian's desk, was a rectangular table covered by a green tablecloth with about twenty chairs around it. On the walls were posters with general information about a famous thinker, author, or book, most of which carried an Islamic content. The same held true for posters and wall hangings in the corridor and courtyard. Most of these were of a Quranic verse or Prophetic Saying, and rather dull in color and presentation. Even when the poster's main content dealt with culture or math, it was appended with Islamic commentary.

The walls of the science lab were decorated with shoddily executed posters about scientific laws or experiments and bore the names of students who made them and the name of their teacher. The wall cupboards contained some rudimentary equipment. In the middle of the lab was a rectangular table with sinks, faucets, and gas pipes, a number of which did not work. The adjoining doctor's room was tidy and clean. It contained a desk and a glass cabinet with some medicines and a first aid kit. On the desk stood a blood pressure monitor and a stethoscope, next to which was a large white ceramic bowl filled with disinfectant. The medicine cabinet contained some medications, bandages, and sealed plastic syringes. Another room that stood out for its cleanliness was the computer and audio-visual aids room which were treated with special care. Curtains protected the equipment from sunlight, electric fans cooled them, and great care was taken to ensure that they remained clean. Students were only allowed in the room when accompanied by the lab attendant, and rarely did they directly handle the equipment.

The remaining three rooms on the first floor were the classrooms of the outstanding students and were undoubtedly the cleanest classrooms of the school. The walls were coated with yellow lime paint, the blackboard was smooth and dark black, and the students' desks were all new. This room was a far cry from the classrooms on the other floors where the desks and chairs were in a state of disrepair, the windowpanes were broken and without curtains, and students were exposed to sun, heat, and cold for long periods of time. Students sometimes hung parts of their clothing over the windows as makeshift curtains. The continual sound of hammering from the neighboring workshops forced the teachers to constantly yell in order to be heard. Each class period thus became a noisy cacophony. The blackboards were faded and when they reflected the sunlight it becomes impossible for those sitting in the rear of the room to read them. Few if any of the light bulbs attached to the wires dangling from the ceiling were functioning, meaning that late classes were essentially held in darkness. Above each blackboard, on the desultory, dirty walls full of holes brought about by acts of student vandalism, hung an unframed portrait of Hosni Mubarak, the president of Egypt.

The other rooms situated around the courtyard included the mosque, canteen, and lavatories. The school mosque was one of the cleanest and most decorated rooms of the school. Its walls were cleanly painted brown (on the lower wall) and yellow (on the upper wall) and filled with wall hangings bearing Quranic verses. In the middle of the *qibla* wall (the side facing Mecca) a *mihrab* (prayer niche) had been painted. Overlooking the coutyard was the school canteen in which packets of biscuits, cakes, soft drinks, and potato chips were sold to the students through a window with iron bars. To the side of the canteen were the student lavatories tiled with white ceramic tiles. Care was taken to keep the five stall lavatories clean, as it was a main inspection point of ministerial delegations when they descended upon the school. In contrast to the tidy student lavatory was a faculty bathroom in disrepair with damaged walls, a leaking faucet, muddied floor, and cracked toilet bowl. In general terms, the school had an air of haphazardness, and reflected a low sense of aesthetics and poverty.

School Governance between Rebellion and Submission

In double-shift schools there is a free hour between shifts. The Boys' School day ended at 12:30 p.m. and the Girls' school began at 1:30 p.m. (In the first term it was the other way around.) During this free hour, custodians erased all traces—dust, garbage, the disarray of the desks and chairs—of the first shift. One felt that they also cleaned away the constant noise and clamor from the boys' shift. Order, discipline, and cleanliness were much more manifest when the girls' shift began, in stark contrast to the seeming chaos of the boys' shift.

The principal of the boys' school, a short unkempt man from the south of Egypt who still retains an Upper Egyptian accent, was highstrung, with marks of exhaustion on his face as he took deep drags of his cigarette. Indecisive and confused when it came to dealing with unforeseen problems, he was often rescued by the advice of three senior teachers in the school who, when not giving their classes, were always in his office. He seemed to have handed over the actual running of the school to these teachers with the longest seniority at the school. Conflicts of interest arose, and the principal's integrity was compromised, from the fact that these teachers invaded positions of power far more extensive than those authorized by work regulations. The principal's integrity was further compromised by widespread rumors that he took kickbacks from teachers who gave private lessons. Private lessons, although officially forbidden, are such a widespread phenomenon that the sum spent on them by Egyptian families has almost become equivalent to the state budget for education (19 billion Egyptian pounds).

The principal resented the education profession and disliked the school to which he moved to two years previously when he was promoted to the office of principal. He became especially furious when follow-up committees sent by higher administrative bodies from the local education district arrived at the school. One might have expected the committees, made up of former teachers and school supervisors, to show solidarity with members of the school administrators, but the senior school administrators consistently exhibited hostility towards them, accusing them of being concerned only with purely formal matters. "They come all high and mighty and harm people, and they've never done a stroke of good work for the school," explained the principal. The committee's main concern did certainly appear to be with formalities and appearances. They spent their time checking things such as the school queue, the cleanliness of the courtyard, the class rosters, the posters in the classrooms, and the presence of the President's photo in each classroom. They also regularly checked the conditions of the lab, the mosque, and the library. Strangely, they did not seem concerned with issues of quality, such as with the performance of teachers.

The boys' school principal expressed frustration with the entire inspection process when he complained, "They make a mountain out of a molehill! Would you believe they complained that the WC wasn't clean, as if everything else in the school is perfect! Give us money and we'll make it sparkle.... They come looking for mistakes. Well, the school and everyone in it can go to hell!" The teachers sitting in the room laughed at his remarks. He further boasted that he could put the inspectors in their place: "You know, when these guys come, I don't budge from my seat. As soon as I see one of them writing in their registers I yell and ask him what kind of rubbish he is writing. I terrify him." In spite of his disorderly appearance and his small physique, the principal's loud, angry voice was capable of intimidating the object of his scorn.

When I asked him about the most pressing problems of his work, he replied in a bored tone as if this was a situation repeating itself for the umpteenth time:

> We're tired of talking and repeating ourselves. The Ministry has taken all powers of authority away from us. You can't bring a student to account or punish him. I can't even make the kids pay the school fees. People here are poor, and even those who have money pretend not to have it. I can't suspend a student until he brings in his father. I

can't punish him, and I can't expel him because we're prohibited from expelling pupils at the basic education level.

When I asked him about problems with the teachers, with the three senior teachers listening in, he answered enthusiastically: "The teachers are excellent. They want to make sweet syrup out of smelly, salty fish."

The time I spent with the principal revealed an administrative style in which passivity and indifference were his weapons against the unrealistic pressures put on him by the surrounding environment. It is plausible that school administrators so bitterly resent the follow-up committees because they represent the oppressor. They seemed to use their positions of seniority to vent some of the pressures to which they themselves are subjected within the overall government bureaucracy. There is a general tendency in Egyptian society for people to act arrogantly towards those whom they see as occupying a lower rung in the social pyramid and to expect their inferiors to address them with the appropriate honorifics. This tendency pervades the structure of social relations in Egyptian society to an even greater extent than in many other societies (Ouda 1995, 180). These situations bring up the issue of resistance versus adaptation in Egyptian behavior. Some hold that throughout their history with all of the trials and tribulations that come with oppression, Egyptians have managed to develop their own unique mechanisms of resistance and, more importantly, of adaptation. Resistance and adaptation have often become so interwoven, with resistance in some instances taking the form of passivity and indifference, that often it seems impossible to place a particular form of social behavior neatly on either side of the adaptation /resistance pendulum (Ouda, 1995, 177).

The principal of the girls' school contrasted sharply to the boys' school principal. Slim and of medium height with a tidy appearance, she rarely smiled, spoke quickly and agitatedly, interacted intelligently with her surroundings, and was capable of providing various justifications for any action she took. As soon as the principal set her foot in the school, she remarked about the level of its cleanliness and gave orders to the custodians in a firm tone. She was highly motivated when it came to improving the aesthetic appearance of the place and the pupils. She kept to the letter of the law, and was anxious to abide by school rules and regulations. Even the follow-up committees commended her work.

When I asked her about the most pressing problems she faced as administrator of the school, she burst out:

I can't punish a pupil...and the profession is in the pits. In the old days a principal was a somebody, but now there's so many of them knocking around. There's no space for the teachers in the school; they sit in the corridors and so the girls overhear their private conversations. We also face the problem that girls coming from primary school don't know how to read or write. They can be absent as often and as long as they like, come back when they feel like it, and I can't expel them because, no sir, this is basic education and expulsion is prohibited. Then we just pass them from year to year until they fail their third preparatory exams (which are held on a national level). I'm held accountable for their results.

In response to my questions about why she found the ministerial follow-up committees so annoying, she said:

They disturb and slow down our work. They only care about negative aspects. They're especially concerned about finding the President's picture hanging in the classroom. They come down really hard on us, and don't show any mercy or consideration of the difficult circumstances we're in. They consider painting the classroom a luxury because there's no money. Fine, OK, but how can they ask for a clean school and at the same time say there's no money? People here are poor. They don't even pay the thirty pound [annual] tuition fee so I can't even get a refurbishment budget.

She seemed to place most of her hopes on the teachers. When I asked her about the teaching staff, she replied: "The teachers are excellent, my handiwork, I trained them. Their attitudes are one and the same with mine." Hers was an administrative style of identification with the place of work. She resented all the laws and decisions issued by the MOE and the local district because she saw these bodies as competing with her over control of the school. Nevertheless, she followed the laws to the letter and held herself responsible for them. Her reference to the teachers as her own "handiwork" is indicative of her proprietary feeling towards the school and its members.

At the same time, she also allowed certain practices to occur which seemed to stand firmly against the spirit and law of formal education, the morning lining-up assembly was one such example. At all Egyptian schools, the day begins with the *taboor*, or student line-up, and in this ritual one can begin to detect how the school culture deviates from the official government text. The students lined up dressed in their blue school uniform, white socks, and shoes made mostly of cheap-looking black fabric or plastic. To a strikingly high degree students donned a white headscarf which covered their chests. Only very few girls—some of the Muslims and all of the Christians—were without headscarves. The *taboor* began with some simple physical exercises to the accompaniment of lively rhythms played on percussion instruments, accordion, and xylophone by a group of girls who were positioned near the flagpole. When the music and movement stopped it was time to listen to the school bulletin which consisted of some Quranic verses, a Prophetic Saying (*hadith*), some news from the day's newspaper on the activities of the president, the First Lady, and the Minister of Education, a religious or patriotic verse, and then the saluting of the flag.

The school's method of saluting the flag caught my attention. Usually, students stand at attention, listen to the national anthem and then, led by the student at the head of the school line, say "Salutations to the Arab Republic of Egypt" (*tahiyya jumhuriyya masr al-arabiyya*) three times. Not so in this school. After listening to the national anthem, the students, led by the school line leader, said:

> Allah is my God, Islam is my religion, Mohammed is my prophet, the Quran is my book, the good deed is my path. O youth of Egypt, O sons of the Nile, this is your flag, the flag of your country, soaring in the sky of glory and liberty. Salute this flag with me. *Allahu Akbar* (God is great), *Allahu Akbar, Allahu Akbar*. Salutations to the Arab Republic of Egypt, Salutations to the Arab Republic of Egypt, Salutations to the Arab Republic of Egypt.

The Christian girls repeated these words alongside their Muslim classmates.

When I asked the principal, who happened to be Christian, about this unusual flag-saluting ceremony, she told me that when she became school principal fifteen years ago the ceremony was already in place and, because of the sensitivity of the situation, it was difficult for her to change it. She added that this particular ritual was masterminded by some of the teachers, and was not the official way of conducting a *taboor*. This flag salutation practice was instituted by Islamists who held sway over some public schools in the 1980s and early 1990s. With the coming to power of the current Minister of Education in 1991, tremendous efforts were made by the Ministry to purge the school environment of extremist Islamist elements (see Herrera, chapter 1). I realized this school's flag saluting ceremony was the result of unofficial negotiations and compromises between officials and the Islamist trend as represented by some teachers and parents. I was especially dismayed by the official silence and acceptance of such a clearly sectarian practice, (particularly by a Christian principal), which seemed to sweep aside nationalist sentiments.

There are some who hold that the Egyptian consciousness—its popular culture and heritage—is deeply rooted in religion. When Egyptians speak of "religion," they mean "Islam" because it is the religion of the majority (El-Saeed 1998, 77). Even as an Egyptian Muslim researcher, it was difficult for me to bring the issue of religion up for discussion during interviews because of the sensitivity of the situation, particularly in light of the timing; my fieldwork took place during the American invasion of Iraq, something which strongly offended Muslim sensibilities and led people to cling ever more firmly to identification with Islam. Throughout its history, Islam has been a tolerant and flexible religion, but it has become more rigid in past decades. It is indeed frightening to think that even those Egyptians who harbor more open and tolerant views are standing by and submitting as those with more rigid and extremist ideas take hold of the country's schools and their youth.

Poverty and Student Performance

The poor tend to distrust official institutions, and indeed lack of trust was one of the most striking characteristics of the parent-school relationship. When a student arrived to school one day after a thirty-day absence, she appeared physically weak and her hair was slightly reddened. Her mother, with sly eyes, tried to justify her daughter's absence by claiming that she had to look after the house while she, the mother, had to stay at a government hospital with her youngest child who had burns and needed an operation. The principal was angry and, without making any effort to mince her words, said to the mother: "This won't do at all. Your daughter is useless. Look at her [poor] grades. What can you say about this?" The mother threatened to go to the Ministry. The principal, after a few moments of silence, agreed to let the girl back into the classroom. After they left the office, the principal commented: "The girl's hair is dyed, they're not really wretched." She cursed the girl and those like her who pull down the score averages of the exams for which she, as principal, is held accountable; she also cursed the ministerial decision prohibiting expulsion of students in the period of basic education. I found it strange how the principal believed that the girl ought to be wretched, that is, ought to show the clear signs of the oppressed person's submissiveness.

In another instance, a student who was failing the year returned to school with her mother after a forty-five-day absence. I conducted an interview with this student to understand her circumstances. She was the second child in a family consisting of two boys and two girls. Her mother was uneducated, divorced, and worked as a seamstress in a clothing factory. Her remarried father worked as a car spray painter and lived in one of Egypt's coastal provinces. He neither visited nor provided for his children with his first wife. Her brothers dropped out of school after sixth grade and took up work in the same craft as their father. Her younger sister was in primary school. Her family lived in one of the one-bedroom apartments of the public housing complex. These are some of her comments in response to my questions about her feelings about school:

> Mom tells me to study about seven times a day. I don't like Social Studies or English, but I like Arabic, Science, and Math. I like the Arabic and Science teachers because they are nice and treat me well, but even so I left school for this period because I was bored. I want to be like Abla[2] Manal, our neighbor, she is good and educated, and her husband works in a factory. She doesn't work, she has good manners, is veiled, keeps to herself, and doesn't get into fights with the neighbors. She and her husband pray, and he never calls her names. I would like to be a doctor.

The last comment about wanting to be a doctor was a bit surprising. She seemed to be reciting to me the official answer she hears all the time in the media and in soap operas, the answer she is supposed to give when asked what she wants to be. And why shouldn't she? After all, she is oblivious of the workings of that infernal machine shaping her.

The principal was in a state of continual struggle: on the one hand, she tried to stick to the standards of the official text of the ministry as embodied in the rules and regulations while, on the other hand, she was unable to improve the standards. She was prone to treating the people of the school as objects. I tried to bring to her attention to the necessity of adopting a spirit of combat. She laughed derisively and asked: "And us, who's going to fight for us?"

Of all the school staff I encountered, it was the school doctor, tenderly receiving her young patients, as a symbol of the spirit of combat.

She dealt with many sick children: very thin boys, girls with drawn faces full of white patches (signs of anemia) looking much younger than their age, children complaining of short-sightedness, stomach pains, headaches and tonsillitis, and children with chronic heart or liver conditions that needed continual follow-up. She told me that parasites, anemia, skin disease, and malnutrition were the most common problems. She shared with me some of her observations about the students and their parents:

> It's a poor neighborhood and the parents are ignorant about health and nutrition. The mass media, which should be playing a role in informing them about nutrition, only addresses the rich. The students here are deprived of the school meal which they need more than students in other schools, but because this is a double-shift school, there's no [time for a] meal. And the girls here, even though they are so weak, sometimes get married right after they finish preparatory school, even though they are ignorant of health and sex-related issues.

When I asked about obstacles she faced, she explained that both the boys and girls were often ill and needed medicine. However, according to regulations, she could not provide medicines costing in excess of four Egyptian pounds per case. The situation was exacerbated by the students' and parents' lack of nutrition and health awareness and lack of extra time in the school day for her to provide health awareness sessions. The school doctor was the only person on the staff to speak directly about the potential harm caused to students by the school's conservative Islamists. In an attempt to help girls learn about their bodies and their health, she initiated some basic sex education courses. Her attempts were thwarted by the principal who, although supportive of the courses in principle, "was afraid of the reactions of some of the backward teachers," or, more specifically, the religious conservatives. A mature, tolerant, and open reading of the world has become a less likely possibility for those people who, in addition to poverty, sickness, and ignorance, are haunted by a ghost even more destructive of human consciousness; religious extremism.

Teaching and Texts

What makes a good teacher? In the pursuit to understand people's perceptions of a good teacher I asked my informants this question straight out. I realized how inane the question was when I kept getting the same answer, albeit phrased differently, from teachers, principals, and inspectors. They answered with some version of the following: "The good teacher is the one who conscientiously delivers information, explains well, fears God in his dealings with students and isn't stingy with explanations." All the answers were couched in the discourse of what Paulo Freire has termed "banking education" (Freire 1970) whereby knowledge is merely deposited into the student's mind. I would argue that this banking education which arose with conditions of modernity, is similar to, and was reinforced by, the pedagogic tradition of the *kuttab* (traditional schools for religious instruction) with its emphasis on memorization and rote-learning.

The students, on the other hand, presented a markedly different explanation of the good teacher. One of them said, "A good teacher is kind to us, solves our problems, cares about us, and is humane." Such answers, in the researcher's opinion, reflect a thirst for the kind of humane environment that the students are deprived of in the context of poverty and oppression surrounding them. I gave up on pursuing direct answers to that question, and decided instead to observe the interactions and events inside the classroom in the hope that they might lead me to something new, or stimulate other questions.

The science class began with the teacher asking the students: "Who will recite the experiment showing how sound travels?" The girls sitting in the front rows raised their hands and pleaded: "Me Miss, Me Miss." The teacher chose a girl who duly recited the steps of the experiment word-by-word from the textbook. Satisfied, the teacher asked the class to applaud her. She then directed her questions to the entire group who responded to her answers in a loud, almost screaming collective voice. She was pleased with her pupils' energy, but did not check that everyone understood. She then asked the class to head to the lab. The girls gathered around the tables, their backs to the walls, and the teacher stood at the blackboard near the video player. She screened an educational film produced by an Egyptian Television educational channel and, while it was running, kept asking: "Which section of the lesson is this?" The collective answer would come to her word-for-word from the textbook. This went on until the class period ended. There was no difference between the teacher's performance style in the classroom and that in the lab, no difference in the students responses either, except that in the class they gave their answers sitting down. The scenario repeated itself in the boys' school, and the same again in another science teacher's class in the girls' school. I wondered about the sacred authority of these texts that took precedence over any real experimentation in the learning process.

A number of ministerial documents stress the importance of science education. Among the stated objectives of the official Curricula of the Preparatory Stage (*Manahij al-Marhala al-'adadiyya*) are to "Accustom students to the practice of scientific thinking and enable them to solve problems they may face in life according to the scientific method that involves analysis and critique," to "train students to employ the necessary precision required in scientific experiments, and to appreciate the efforts of scientists," and to "deepen religious ideas and the sense of God's greatness and omnipotence" (Arab Republic of Egypt 2003, 118–119). The phraseology in which these goals are couched cries out for discourse analysis, but for the purposes of this paper it is enough to throw some light on the disparities between official texts and actual practices. The classroom scenes previously described provide commentary enough on the first two goals. As for the third goal, it reflects a general orientation in the teaching of all subjects and explains why the school textbook in each subject often includes a Quranic verse related in some way to the lesson unit.

With regard to math, the MOE curriculum guidelines state: "Attention in Math should be given to such methods as dialogue, discussion, deduction, and to independent learning." It goes on that:

> The students should be trained to undertake practical exercises in geometry and to master its tools and should be given numerous examples of each theory taught. . . . In addition to the textbook, teaching aids appropriate to the lesson should be used for explanation and student assessment in the classroom. (Arab Republic of Egypt 2003 118–119)

In actuality the job of math teachers was reduced to explaining the theorem and its proofs. During math class, the teacher would ask one of the students sitting in the front to come to the board to solve a problem. These teachers were like cars without gear boxes, explaining at a single speed without taking into consideration disparities in levels of understanding or attention among their students. Many of the students gave up on following the lesson, chatted, slept, or goofed around instead.

I asked one of the most senior math teachers at the boys' school, a man with a vicious tongue, who was at times extremely severe in his treatment of students, "Are you a successful teacher?" His answer was:

"Yes. The boys understand the classes they take with me and like me even though I am tough on them. I come down hard on them, but it's in their interest."

When I asked him for his opinion on the students at his school, he replied:

> They vary, depending on their background. The majority, though, are from wretched backgrounds, from ignorant families without money to buy supplementary books or to join study groups. The whole area is garbage; craftsmen, hash dens, and play stations. I print the monthly exams at my own expense. The boys here aren't interested in their studies. They work as microbus drivers and in workshops and shops.

This teacher's mere presence in the courtyard or the corridor was enough to strike terror in the students' hearts and to make a bit of order prevail. But his teaching performance was no different from that of the others.

When I asked an English teacher about the level of her students she answered, "The ones with educated parents know how to read well, but the rest aren't great because most of the people living in the area are uneducated." Another said, "The good students attend study groups." This teacher was harsher in her treatment of the students than other teachers. She began every class with a two-minute exam to see whether the girls had memorized the words or not. She immediately marked them. Most exams were below passing grade. If, during class time, a student answered a question incorrectly the teacher sent her to the back of the classroom where she had to stand facing the wall.

In terms of teaching methods, the Arabic classes in the boys' and girls' schools followed a similar method. One topic in an Arabic class in the girls' school was an essay by the literary and education reform figure from the early twentieth century, Taha Hussein, entitled "Justice." The teacher's presentation was neutral and she made no attempt to make connections with real life events. This teacher, clothed in conservative Islamic dress, provided very selective (and to my understanding distorted), examples from Arab Islamic heritage to explain the meaning of justice and injustice. I asked a student what she understood from her teacher's class about justice and she responded, "It means the punishment of murderers and thieves according to divine law."

In a social studies class held at the boys' school, the teacher began by writing "Egypt between the two wars" on the blackboard. She also wrote the main points of the lesson. When she mispronounced a foreign name and a student, not understanding her, asked "Who?" she got angry and told him to "Go outside." Her lesson consisted in repeating the sentences and paragraphs of the textbook without making any connections between the events narrated and more recent or contemporary events.

In the library class at the boys' school, a mandatory subject designed to get students to read on their own, I found the teacher handing out copies of *Sahih Al-Bukhari*, a text from the Islamic canon. When I asked the teacher if his choice was based on student interest, his reply was that he was the one who made the decisions, adding that the name Bukhari was mentioned in their Arabic readers and Islamic religion textbooks as the source of Prophetic says. He said they wanted to know more about Bukhari. The teacher wrote the title of the lesson on the blackboard: "General Knowledge and Religious Culture." When I asked him to let them choose a topic for themselves, he answered: "This is a generation that doesn't read." Nevertheless, the students asked him many question including how to perform the prayer for the dead, what happens in the grave, and how a person could be resurrected in one piece if he was run over by a train. In response to the question "How can we know about events taking place in the grave if we haven't seen any proof of them?" the teacher offered, "This is one of the things we should take on faith, accept without thought." The class ended without the teacher taking up the thread offered by the last question in order to give the students a glimpse of what is called critical thinking, the importance of which is emphasized ad nauseam at every conference, symposium, and paper and in every book assigned in the faculties of education which produced all those teachers.

Conclusion: Subsistence Education

Teachers and pupils perceive their reality through two contrasting texts simultaneously: on the one hand is the official reality as it is presented and depicted in formal texts, and on the other hand is the impoverished reality in the grip of which they find themselves and which they are ashamed to admit. Fictions about the social, cultural, and material reality of schools are perpetuated, in part, through government-approved texts which teachers transmit in the classroom, usually without commentary, cross-referencing, elaboration, or connection to their lives or the lives of their pupils. It is as if these texts are Holy Writ and not open to discussion. Members of the school administration, when they are not passive and disinterested in the school community, are also complicit in perpetuating an image incongruous with reality. They try to maintain an image of pupils and teachers as happy, and brightly painted objects in an imagined pristine and beautiful school, despite the heaps of dirt and debris covering the school walls, the holes disfiguring the classrooms, not to mention the demoralized psychological state of students and teachers.

The teachers' treatment of the students, from ignoring those in the back row, or treating them as a single body at which questions are thrown, erase the individuality of each student. By not acknowledging their individuality, teachers, in a sense, deny students their humanity. The students often perceive of themselves and their families in an inferior manner, in congruence with their teachers' judgments of them. The teachers' feelings of incapacity, their constant fear of being punished, their lack of self-confidence, and avoidance of confrontation, all represent features of the oppressed class. These modes of internalized oppression lead to a lack of social and cognitive competencies and an avoidance of the new and unfamiliar, since anything untested and new becomes a cause for anxiety (Hegazy 43–44).[3]

Education in Egypt continues to be in high demand for it is the Egyptian people's last line of defense in the face of social marginalization. Despite the fact that education at all levels is pyramidal in nature and tends to reproduce social stratification, it still provides many Egyptians hope for opportunities and social mobility. In reality parents learn to expect only the bare minimum—to expect a subsistence education whereby their children learn to read and write or, at best, to qualify for a technical trade school. A parent commented: "If the boy doesn't get an education he'll be pushed around for the rest of his life." A female student remarked: "I want to be a mother who knows how to read and write." And a male student stated: "I want an education so that I don't wind up working in a mechanic's workshop and get beaten up all the time." This school—a subsistence education school—offers the modest services demanded of it, and not much else. In keeping with their sense of incapacity and inertia, the teachers, supervisors, and principals, make no effort to offer alternative pedagogic visions. Education in this autocratic atmosphere represents a political contract between the state and its subjects, whereby the former offers to the latter free certificates without education in return for compliance and gratitude.

Notes to Chapter 3

1. Henry Giroux, for example, shows how the relation between the school and society is complicated, for not only do the students rebel against the official ideology imposed on them, but they also form a counterculture and environment in which different social practices are produced. Although Giroux does not claim that students have the final say regarding what they consider anomalous in the social structure, he affirms that the excess of resistance represented by the students allows for the existence of a powerful, albeit limited, space in which new forms of power may emerge (Giroux 1983, xi–xii).

2. *Abla* is a respectful term denoting sister and may be used for older sisters, relatives and nonrelatives, and is also used for teachers.

3. The work of Pierre Bourdieu is also relevant in this context. Bourdieu emphasizes the concept of class spirit as habitus, "a system of shared social dispositions and cognitive structures which generates perceptions, appreciations and actions," which is internalized from early childhood (Bourdieu 1988, 279). Bourdieu shows how educational systems work at consolidating and reproducing a habitus through pedagogic communication, something manifested in this ethnographic study.

References

Al-Issawi, Ibrahim Hassan. 1989. *Nahw Khareeta Tabaqiya li-Masr: Al-Ishkaliyat Al-Nazariya wa'l Iqtirab Al-Manhaji min Al-Waqei' Al-Tabaqi Al-Missri* [Towards a Class Map of Egypt: Theoretical Problems and Methodological Approaches towards the Reality of the Egyptian Class Structure]. Cairo: Al-Markaz Al-Qawmi li'l- Buhuth Al-'Ijtima'iya wa'l-Jina'iya.

Arab Republic of Egypt, Ministry of Education. 2000. *Manahij Al-Marhala Al-I'dadiya* [Preparatory Level Curricula]. Cairo: The Ministry of Education.

Arab Republic of Egypt. 2003. *Manahij al-Marhala al-I'dadiyya* [Curricula of the Preparatory Stage]. Cairo: Ministry of Education.

Bourdieu, Pierre. 1988. *Homo Academicus*. Cambridge: Polity Press.

El-Saeed, Rifaat. 1998. *Al-Yassar, Al-Dimoqrati wa'l-Ta'aslum* [The Left, Democracy, and Islamization]. Cairo: Mo'assassat Al-Ahali.

Freire, Paulo. 1970. *Pedagogy of the Oppressed*. New York: Continuum, 1970.

Freire, Paulo. 1998. *Teachers as Cultural Workers*. Trans. Donaldo Macedo. Boulder, CO: Westview Press.

Giroux, Henry A. 1983. *Theory and Resistance in Education: A Pedagogy for the Opposition*. New York: Bergin and Garvey.

Hegazy, Mostafa. 1986. *Al-Takhaluf Al-Ijtima'i: Madkhal illa Saikolojiyat Al-Insan Al-Maqhoor* [Social Underdevelopment: An Approach to the Psychology of the Oppressed]. Lebanon: Ma'had Al-Inmaa' Al-'Arabi.

Ouda, Mahmoud. 1995. *Al-Takayuf wa'l-Muqawama: Al-Juzour Al-'Ijtima'iya wa'l-Siyassiya l'il-Shakhsiya Al-Massriya* [Adaptation and Resistance: The Social and Political Roots of the Egyptian Character]. Cairo: Al-Majliss Al-A'la l'il-Thaqafa.

Spindler, George D. (Editor) 1997. *Education and Cultural Process: Anthropological Approaches*. Long Grove, Ill: Waveland Press.

United Nations Development Program (UNDP). 2002. *Arab Human Development Report 2002: Creating Opportunities for Future Generations*. New York: United Nations Publications.

United Nations Development Program (UNDP). 2003. *Arab Human Development Report 2003: Building a Knowledge Society*. New York: United Nations Publications.

4

A Great Vocation,
a Modest Profession:
Teachers' Paths and Practices

IMAN FARAG

Summary

Education in Egypt has long been treated as a cornerstone of national development and a paramount social wager. At the same time its principal actors, namely teachers, have been consistently denigrated. Teachers tend to be blamed for society's inability to reach an adequate standard of development and have become society's scapegoats. In other words, the actors have not risen to the level and importance of the wager. This chapter traces national debates about teachers from the liberal age of the 1920s to the neoliberalism of the 1990s. Unlike the expert literature on teaching, the focus here is on the actual and discursive practices and paths teachers follow to resolve and overcome the contradiction between the profession and the vocation. Through teacher interviews it addresses the questions:

- Where do teachers stand between the greatness of their vocation on the one hand, and the actual conditions in which their profession is practiced, on the other?

- What strategies do teachers resort to in order to narrow the gap between the modesty of the profession, and the greatness of the vocation?

To Be Educated....

Irrigation and education have constituted the basis for the foundation of modern Egypt in both material and symbolic terms. The copious symbolic and material resources allotted to education, whether by the government or by ordinary families who invest in education as a means of fulfilling their dreams for the future, testify to its importance. Education, thus, is a powerful tool of political control, whether as a tool for dreams, or a tool for liberation. To be precise, knowledge liberates while the institution controls: such is the structural problematic.

Education plays a critical role in nation building and in the production of the citizen by force. Political and social rights are related to, and dependent upon, the acquisition of a parallel amount of schooling. Even the minimal ability needed to negotiate and demand one's rights requires some level of schooling. It follows, then, that those who have not gone through the formal school system are distanced from the possibilities of citizenship. Education, thus, is the link connecting the individual to the state, or the system of duties dictated by citizenship in return for rights. In European societies, by contrast, it was not education but work that served as the basis of the political link between citizenship and rights. As Robert Castel puts forward in the case for France, modern citizenship shifted from the question of poverty to the right to work (1995). In Egyptian society, it has been the question of education that has solidified the link between the citizen and the state and has served as the pillar upon which all other rights are founded (Farag 1999).

The notion that education represents the pillar of all rights can be better expressed by borrowing and altering the famous dictum of the National Charter (1961), the ideological document par excellence for the socialist transition years during which the pan-Arabist leader, Gamal Abdel Nasser, was president. Its claim that Work is a right, work is honor, work is a duty becomes, "Education is a right, education is honor, education is a duty." Some might hold that such sixties slogans, whether to do with work or education, belong to the past. What concerns us here is that even though the connection between work, income, and educational levels largely weakened following the economic Open Door Policies of the 1970s (*infitah*), and the gap between the desire to continue education and the ability to do so widened, the symbolic importance of the wager of education remained intact.

To Be a Teacher....

Most teachers work in government schools and are therefore government employees. Yet one could argue that teachers differ from other government employees insofar as they are expected to perform a social role based on self-dedication and to act as moral authorities in society. Due to the centrality of the teacher's vocation for societal advancement, their low salaries are perceived as especially scandalous. Why, then, are teachers not sharing in the prestige of the important social endeavor of education? Why do teachers appear more as objects than as subject-actors? Why, in the discourse of social criticism, do teachers appear as a problem, if not the problem? It is as if teachers are to blame for society's inability to reach an adequate standard of development. In other words, the actors have not risen to the level and importance of the wager. Teachers have become society's scapegoats.

Teachers: From the Liberal Age to Neoliberalism

The discrepancy between the importance of the wager (education) and the importance of the actors (teachers) has historical roots dating back to the 1920s. Although the current situation is undoubtedly different, the past provides clues to understanding some contemporary dynamics of the teaching profession. Certain current attitudes about teachers can be traced to the "Liberal Age," the period between the adoption of the 1923 Constitution and the Free Officer's coup d'état in July 1952. This period of state-building was characterized by such political features as a multiparty political system, constitutional culture, and freedom of expression alongside authoritarian political interventionism by the British occupation and the Egyptian monarch. It was also a formative period for major modern educational institutions including the National University (1925), and the Institute of Pedagogy (1929).

In 1937, a graduate of the Higher School for Teachers and principal of the Maqasid Government Primary School in Tanta, Ali Hassan El-Hakei, wrote about the incongruent perceptions of teachers during this period. In his book, *The Problems of Education in Egypt* (*Mushkilat Al-Tarbiya fi Misr*), El-Hakei argues that teachers in modern schools neither enjoyed the status of the traditional (religious) educator and transmitter of knowledge, nor did they carry the status of other professions. As he puts it: "Next to the great appreciation for the teacher, you find a silent repressed view that is denigrating and colored by pity; it is only the teacher and none of his fellow professionals who suffers from this ambiguous attitude." He attributes the teacher's declined status, in part, to the "boredom...of being a student" (8), and also to the ways in which teaching is unrealistically inflated by commentators distant from the profession. He notes:

> According to public opinion, teachers are said to be as prestigious as men of religion; in fact their influence remains far from that of politicians, financiers, lawyers, doctors, and other professionals in touch with public life. It could be that public opinion as exemplified by the daily papers, print media, and pulpits, is monopolized by social classes far from the atmosphere of teaching like lawyers and men of letters. They have their eloquence...and a special magical connection with public opinion, a connection for which the worn out teacher has no time to build up through publicity and research. (6–7)

El-Hakei, a former teacher who was promoted to the high professional rank of school principal, attempted to spread a new notion of education in order to revise the public image of the teacher. He also tried to understand the apparent dissatisfaction many teachers exhibited towards their profession:

> ...The Egyptian teacher...does not like his profession and does not work at improving it as does his French or German counterpart....How many Egyptian teachers planned to master teaching as soon as they finished their secondary education? I know that in most cases the teacher resorts to a teachers college only after the doors to other colleges have been shut....I have found only one case that calls for admiration and respect, the case of a teacher who was with me in Damietta whose resources qualified him to pursue other directions but who, out of love and eagerness, preferred the teaching profession....(71)

Governmental education at that time was limited to a small minority who could afford the fees, and government schools often surpassed private schools in quality and teacher privileges. The teaching profession was organized around cultural and professional societies and leagues that were highly hierarchical; teachers became members of a given society based on the school from which they graduated. In other words, the institution in which the teacher received his/her tertiary education certificate, whether a teachers' training institute, an Arabic language school, the Institute of Pedagogy, and so on, carried an inherent ranking within the overall profession. The profession produced clearly defined boundaries and hierarchies. Elementary school teachers, the majority of teachers, were de facto at the bottom of the hierarchy and received the brunt of the liberal era's class snobbery.

By the 1960s, as Egypt experimented with a one-party system under the charismatic leadership of Gamal Abdul-Nasser, formal education underwent a dramatic change. Questions pertaining to mass education were reformulated, and teacher training and schooling at all levels experienced a vast expansion. Education, along with agrarian reform, nationalization, and regulations of work conditions, was considered a means for the realization of social justice, not to mention access to public sector and government jobs. Consequently, the free primary education that started in the 1940s, extended to include higher education in 1962. The ideal type Egyptian from that period would have been a young, educated engineer from a poor peasant family, who gained a higher social status thanks to free education and agrarian reform.

The late educational historian who wrote on education during that period, Mohamed Abu El-Asaad, underscores the incompatibility of socialist principles of equity with the conditions of teachers because teachers received the lowest salaries of all state employees. He writes:

> If the teacher has always been at the bottom of the class ladder in capitalist society, will he remain so in socialist society? And how can we leave the fingerprints of capitalism and feudalism on one hundred and twenty thousand [teachers] when we are asking them to bring up our new generations according to the ideas, principles, and goals of socialism? (59)

The famous secular philosopher and specialist of English literature, Lewis Awad (1914-1990), also sheds light on the conditions of the teaching profession during that era. In *Al-Jam'a w'al-Mujtama' al-Jadeed (The University and the New Society)*, he balks at dehumanizing notions that link teaching to economic growth. He writes:

> To tie...teaching...with the...national economy, such that if one expands so does the other and if one shrinks so does the other, does not only constitute an assault on human rights, but is a form of human and social degeneration. (1964, 37)

As an advocate of humanistic education, he draws attention to the bias of universities towards the natural sciences:

> The State's exaggerated respect for scientific culture and technology, a respect which has led to the absorption of the secondary schools' best graduates into faculties of science with their most backward students being sent off to faculties of humanities, has led to a grave imbalance because it has flooded the colleges of humanities with failures. (44)

Awad's liberal view is not void of elitism or bias: he associates creative abilities in the humanities with theoretical studies. Awad also postulates on how branches of knowledge are ranked and why specializations that are officially touted as being of great nobility and importance, that is, teaching, are positioned in low ranks. More importantly, he shows how this ranking is widely accepted as if it were natural, logical, and even fair.

Within the teaching profession, hierarchies persist in which teachers who graduate from top colleges enjoy more prestige than graduates of teacher-training institutes who are stigmatized for their low academic background. This brings us to the second and more problematic strand of Awad's argument, which is that he calls for no less than doing away with colleges of education in favor of making the faculties of arts and sciences responsible for educating primary and secondary school teachers. He proposes that teacher-training institutes be appended to universities in order to provide graduate level training in pedagogy even though he regards studies in pedagogy as unnecessary. He argues that teachers do not need to take courses to specifically learn how to teach because:

> We do not teach an engineer, doctor, or economist, on top of his specialization in engineering, medicine, or economics, how to be an engineer or doctor or economist; it is enough that each be a human being knowledgeable of the ethics of his profession. (165)

Awad's arguments can be placed in a broader suspicion of teacher training as representing colonial interests.[1]

Public debates about teachers and teacher education take a somewhat different turn in the 1990s, which witnessed transformations of the education market, as illustrated by the following vignette. In August of 1998, a major Egyptian newspaper advertised a contest for fifty thousand teaching jobs in the capital city, Cairo. Some two hundred seventy-five thousand people ventured to Cairo, many from the provinces, and security forces had to be brought in to organize the crowd. The reactions to this peculiar teacher employment contest were varied. Some recorded their dismay at why such a huge number of people should greedily pounce upon such modest-paying jobs. Graduates from the Islamic Al-Azhar university saw the contest as blatantly discriminatory, as it was only open to graduates of the secular national universities. But it seemed to be the free market discussion that resounded most loudly in the press. This was a time in which the neoliberal atmosphere promoting private profit-making enterprises, with the young business entrepreneur as exemplar, prevailed. Hence, many scoffed at the show of so many people who preferred a government job—with its modest salaries, but important guarantees and securities—to the magic of capitalist ventures. Other commentators pointed out that those seeking teaching jobs were not actually after the teaching job, per se, but after the private lessons, which de facto became available with teaching. The job applicants viewed things differently. The contest was not only open to graduates of education faculties, but graduates of all faculties. Those with degrees in education were led to wonder what special privilege their degrees held because they were supposed to be promised, on graduation, the equivalent of a tenured teaching contract.[2]

Although the government had been backing away from tenure policies for education college graduates, the teaching sector still makes up the lion's share of governmental employment. The significance of the government job itself, however, has changed, as individuals have had to take on two or more jobs to attain some acceptable living standard. The income derived from the government job has come to constitute a spare income associated with some security, and, at the same time, limited work hours allowing for engagement in other less secure, but more profitable jobs. From this perspective it appears that market relations—which include the lucrative industry of private lessons—have come to dominate the educational process.

Private lessons, which represent an interpenetration of the official job with the private activity, may be considered a form of class struggle taking place on the educational terrain, one which contains nonethical means and ends. This struggle has been left to the mechanisms of the market and has essentially led to a privatization of part of the education sector in the context of a society driven towards economic liberalism without a minimum level of social rights. The dominance of market relations over the educational process, in other words, constitutes the main—if not the only—shadow over the teacher's profession, and controls the mechanisms of social struggle, regardless of the intentions of those involved in it. A teacher expresses this idea in the following terms: "If there were no private lessons or study groups, then the word 'teachers' would equal 'a group of beggars.'" Parents, a topic that, in and of itself, calls for research, participate in the rules of the game that they unwittingly perpetuate.

Clearly, the teaching profession has been negatively affected by these market trends. Moreover, it seems that the vocational dimension of the profession has been against the current. For whether we view teaching with the criteria of competency (professional) or equity (social), it would seem that what is asked and expected of teachers is contrary to the wave of neoliberal tendencies.

Teachers' Voices

If we take media coverage as a yardstick, it is clear that education is among the most important, if not the most important, social issue of the day. How, then, does it transpire that teachers' voices are persistently absent in the media? Instead, members of various specializations (especially those whose names are preceded by the magical letters "D and r.") dominate the discussions. To address this discrepancy, the following part of this study is based on interviews with Egyptian teachers.[3] Generally speaking, interviews have a special significance because they can enable us to adopt and make use of the subjects' language and unique expressions to reformulate public discourse.

I conducted interviews with eight teachers from August to October, 2003. This sample, which includes one female and seven male teachers who work at the primary, preparatory, and secondary levels, and who have from seven to forty years of professional experience, can be described as varied.[4] All the teachers who participated in this study did so out of their desire to serve knowledge and to help research concerned with the issue of teaching, a motivation they find worthy. It must also be said that the teachers were highly recommended to me by parents and colleagues, making those in this sample a special kind of teacher. What distinguishes them from other teachers is their commitment to the ethics of the profession, or their unconventional—compared to their colleagues—interests, like creative writing, involvement in public service, or their desire to someday teach at the university level.

For the most part, these teachers experience feelings of intellectual isolation. Something as simple as reading a newspaper sometimes sets them apart from their colleagues. One teacher, who reads the somewhat highbrow newspaper, *Al-Ahram Al-Iqtasadi* (The *Al-Ahram* periodical on economics), was cause for his colleagues' astonishment. They would tell him, "You're better off saving the money you spend on this paper to prepare for marriage." They would mock him by saying that he's living in the wrong era and should have lived a the time when a teacher "belonged to the Wafd Party and knew Al-Mutanabbi's poetry by heart."[5] Another teacher told how his colleagues were surprised to see him reading *Al-Hayat* newspaper (a daily pan-Arab newspaper catering to intellectuals) since it contains no sports or crime articles, instead of the more commonly read papers, *Al-Gumhouriya* and *Al-Akhbar*" (the lightest semi-official daily papers).

The often low cultural level of teachers has clear consequences for students. A former principal relates the story of a teacher who had not heard of the celebrated modern Arab novelist Yusif Idris. When this teacher had to teach a required lesson on the author, he dismissed the widely acclaimed short story, "A Glance," as being by "some writer. . . . His name is Yusif Idris. . . . A Communist infidel . . . the whole story is about this girl, a servant carrying a tray of potatoes on her way to the bakery. . . . " This teacher could not have possibly communicated an appreciation of literature to his students. On the contrary, he was more likely to convey attitudes of distain for Arabic literature. The principal goes on to complain how some teachers have such a low scientific and cultural level that they transmit their superstitions to the students. A female teacher, for example, quite seriously told her noisy class that if they didn't keep quiet that she would make the *jinn* (spirits) take over.

The teachers I interviewed expressed disappointment and at times derision at the low cultural level of their colleagues, however their views should not be understood as elitist. For in many respects these teachers share a common cultural terrain with their colleagues, such as the realm of popular culture—for example, watching football matches. Rather, their positions appear to be a combination—difficult to interpret, but seemingly prevalent— of sympathy, paternalism, disappointment, and frustration towards what they consider a loss of the bare minimum of qualities with which a teacher should be endowed.

Many of the teachers stressed that they consider themselves outside the norm and therefore not fit to be in a sample. I cannot incontestably prove that these teachers are more committed or different from other teachers. However, I highly suspect they are, and this factor limits the possibility of generalizing this study's findings, though by no means does it render these teachers' voices less important. Indeed, their voices may be even more important.[6]

In my role as a researcher, I approached the teachers as informed, knowledgeable subjects, and listened to their experiences, complaints, and worries sympathetically. It was apparent that none of them had ever been the subject of this kind of interest before, and if some of the material in this research paper hits the nail on the head, it is due to the novelty of the experience for the subjects and the researcher alike. Prior to this experience, my own knowledge of teachers' circumstances had, been limited to information gleaned through secondary sources, including historical literature (much of which overlaps with common stereotypes about teachers), and the experience (not always easy to recall), of being a student. Unlike the expert literature on teaching, my focus here is on the actual and discursive practices and paths teachers follow to resolve and overcome the contradiction between the profession and the vocation.

The First Class

I asked the teachers' to share their memory of their first class assuming the following: the recollection of this presumably decisive experience would allow us to understand the image the teacher had of himself at the start of his career. Did this stage have special significance, and would this significance disappear under the pressure of daily complications, routine performance, and habit? Some teachers had forgotten this moment and tried to go back in time to remember it, while others were neither concerned with the question nor could they see the importance of answering it. Still others went into great detail and delved into an extremely private realm.

Some teachers recalled their youthfulness and how they tried to establish a rapport with their young wards. One remembered his sense of identification with the students and recalled:

> I was not much older than the students. It was a situation of *School of Trouble-Makers (Madrasit Al-Mushaghebeen*, a very popular comic play that ran for several years in the 1970s and is often shown on television). I tried to befriend them and would share my cigarettes with them.

A Cairene, whose first teaching job was in a remote agricultural area, relates experiences of physical and cultural distance:

> I remember my first class very well because it took me two hours to reach the school on public transport. I even had to take open-top vans. I was in a celebratory mood and wearing my best clothes. The students were in awe of me because I was a teacher from Cairo. I introduced myself, 'my name is so and so, and I want to get to know you, I'll be teaching you Social Studies.' I was afraid of failing. It was as if I was the one sitting for an exam, not them. They took a week, hesitant about whether or not to trust me, and for a week I did not yell at them.

Another teacher recalls walking into a noisy class and trying to insist on more respectful behavior from them.

> I was silent till they quieted down," he explains. "They began to feel that there was a teacher in the classroom. Smiles were exchanged. I greeted them and said I am your brother So and So, and of course 'brother' has a special ring." He pointed out that the first class at the beginning of any school year is always "the first class" because "even if the teacher is an old-timer, the students are new, and limits have to be drawn from the first class.

Another teacher, who went into the profession reluctantly, recalls his first day at an over-crowded boys' school in an industrial neighborhood in Cairo where he also made sure on his first day to set the rules for behavior:

> I hadn't slept well the night before. I had taken this job [as an eighth grade teacher] only because of my parents' wishes for me to have a secure job and study for my master's degree afterwards. The class was on the first floor, the fifth classroom on the right. I didn't know what I was going to say. Part of my fear was due to my coming in the middle of the school year. I walked in to find huge looking boys, more than fifty of them, and some of them without chairs, sitting on wooden planks resting between two chairs. I felt that this was the decisive moment: if they felt I was defeated or afraid I wouldn't be able to change their impression. I looked at them and kept silent. I remembered the values of long ago, how it was a sign of respect for students to stand up when our teachers entered the room. I waited five, seven minutes, until they stood up. After that I tried briefly to introduce myself and said in a formal way: 'I will be cooperating with you to continue with Mr. So and So's efforts.' Most of them had

good attitudes, but some were rebellious, not concerned with taking notes because they were taking private lessons with another teacher. That was my impression. Others at least were correct in their behavior. I looked into their eyes, read not just their words, but their expressions. I tried to stay in control that day. I kept the lesson a two-way affair so that the students would stay awake and not daydream and I moved around a lot. I didn't know them and didn't know about teaching, but I had some ideas. I would pick on the boys sitting next to those who seemed careless or brutish, as a way of keeping an eye on them. From the first class I was convinced that I wouldn't continue teaching, but at least I though I would learn while I was there.

Another teacher told how he, like so many other new teachers, was placed in a problem class of trouble-makers. He recalled how he dealt with the fear of having to control a gang of brutish boys, and why he regrettably felt he had to resort to violence to assert his authority:

> They gave me the most difficult class of 'trouble-makers.' It included the failures and those with health problems. The percentage of Copts was supposedly high in this class. I overheard a teachers say, 'the big chief—[the senior teacher]—threw the trash classroom to him.' The floor tiles were broken, there were no windows, and the class was extremely overcrowded. When over twenty-five students are sitting on the floor it's impossible to say 'let him sit next to you.' My anxiety made me move about more and more quickly and ask questions and answers at random. The bigger boys were the trouble-makers, and I told myself I had to hit someone. I was more afraid than they were. I picked on the most trouble-making student, who, as chance would have it, was the hugest boy in the class.... I hit him with the principal's cane.... After shaming the strongest one, I didn't need to hit again. After that I befriended the boys who were serious about their studies, and the one I hit pretended to befriend me. It was a violent and unpleasant experience.

The theme of control, and lack thereof, came up frequently. An Arabic language teacher remembers with embarrassment how he lost control of his first class and walked out of it midway, forcing the principal to take his place. By relying on outside help, teachers appear incompetent. But what channels exist beyond the classroom for dealing with problems? There appears to have been a clear sense among teachers that some situations call for outside intervention, however there was a difference of opinion regarding just when the teacher's responsibility ended and that of the administration began.

Despite their variety, the answers testify to a common element, namely the teachers' conviction of the necessity of defining the rules of the game from the first moment, as if they were the ones in control of the game. But are the rules of the game set by the teacher? And do the rules change with a change of the class?

On Control

The job of the teacher, as succinctly defined by one of the interviewees, is to impart knowledge and maintain control. These tasks seem far from the comprehensive ideal of teachers as the raisers of the nation's children and youth. Teachers are faced with the daunting task every day, of having to control, punish, rear, and transmit knowledge during a forty-five minute class period with sixty or more students. The teacher is supposed to control himself and his tongue, not to give rein to feelings of anger and frustration, to be objective and fair and not show favoritism, to live up to the role of the mature leader in appearance, words, and behavior, to put aside his personal worries, and to undertake the required paperwork that would allow others (inspectors and supervisors) to make sure that he performed the task required of him. Last but not least, teachers are expected to transmit the official knowledge of the textbooks. There is no doubt that the education and teaching which takes place in the classroom, is a complicated process with interwoven dimensions. I tried to understand what dimensions and techniques teachers used to cope in the classroom.

Most of the teachers agree that the most effective class is the one that is run like a Swiss watch, one where you can hear a pin drop. A well-controlled class, they explain, is in the best interest of the student, for his/her main objective is to retain the maximum amount of information and earn high grades on the exams. To maintain control, teachers often organize their classes according to a fixed formula. A secondary school teacher explains, for example, that he divides his classes into three parts: five minutes of questions about the previous lesson; thirty-five minutes of discussion and dialogue about the lesson subtopics; and five minutes of questions about the lesson itself. The teacher finds that this division of time, which he upholds even with as many as sixty students in the class, "makes the teaching process successful."

Yet it takes much more than a well-organized lesson to control a class; it also takes a certain approach to discipline and punishment. When discussing aspects of discipline, teachers often raise the issue of corporal punishment. Hitting, most commonly in the form of caning a student on the palms, is prohibited by the Ministry of Education (MOE) but remains a widespread practice. One of the teachers speaks bitterly about the MOE prohibition on hitting, saying that forbidding the teacher to hit the student is "the last nail in the teacher's coffin" because "the teacher has no rights where the student is concerned: no dismissal, no hitting, no verbal abuse; so all that's left is the use of grades." The use of physical punishment appears widespread and regarded as a part of the normal daily interaction between teacher and student.

Does the word "violence" have meaning when it becomes an ordinary practice undertaken with the agreement of all the parties participating in it? I asked the teachers if violence (i.e., corporal punishment), constitutes a momentary lapse by the teacher or whether it is considered an accepted practice. One teacher explains how the cane represents a threat and can help to keep students in check. He says:

> I do not hit, but I find myself carrying a cane like all the other teachers. I convinced myself that I was carrying it to use for pointing at the blackboard, whereas in principle if you're carrying a cane it means you can use it to hit.

A female secondary school teacher speaks about the importance of students knowing the possibility of physical punishment. She explains:

> I pull the girl's hair slightly, half seriously, half in jest, and say 'Show us whether or not you've washed your hair,' and the girls laugh. If I don't do this, they'll say the class is boring. Unfortunately, this has become the rule.

Another teacher finds himself drifting with the current towards prevalent punitive practices:

> Sometimes I hit," [he explains], "a light punch, almost in jest. But the boy feels it is because I have his best interests at heart. The other students calm him down, absorb his anger because they know I am a serious teacher. But sometimes students ally themselves against a teacher. But the student will accept anything from the good

teacher.... For forty years of my life I have not faced the situation of
a student complaining about me or hitting me.

On the issue of control and differential approaches to boys and girls,
a young, optimistic teacher at a coeducational school, says: "I treat the
girls better than the boys, and this is because I want to control any mas-
culine tendencies I might have and because girls are more likely to
undergo oppression."

A teacher with forty years experience states: "Girls are very pleasant,
and teaching them is easier than teaching boys" yet teachers feel they
need to be more delicate with female students. "There is more freedom
with the boys," a teacher explains, "With the girls I have to watch what I
say." The relation between the male teacher and the postadolescent
female student can also be tense, as one teacher points out. "Girls fall in
love with their teachers and choose teachers as fiancés. When they gather
round me, I, as a man from the village, try to preserve a distance. If I
merely raise my hand, it might brush against her." Another male teacher
explains that he couldn't let even a seven-year-old girl student kiss him
(in greeting on the cheek) since he would risk accusations. "I have to
create barriers."

Some teachers consciously avoid negative confrontations with students by maintaining an open, friendly, and stimulating atmosphere
inside and outside the classroom. Yet, they face certain barriers having to
do mainly with lack of class time and lack of interest on the part of students. A philosophy teacher notes. "I like to speak with my students
about other subjects, but where are the students who are interested in
other subjects? All they want to talk about is [personal] relationships and
other such trivia." Another said that he enjoys talking about other matters in the classroom, but given the packed curriculum, finds little time
to do so.

For those teachers who prefer not to hit, they resort to other forms
of punishment. One teacher suspends his students from sports, but said
his students say they would rather be hit and get the punishment quickly
over. Other teachers try to use tactics such as shaming or teasing the student, as one teacher describes:

If I'm emotional, I try as much as possible not to hit. I think before
hitting. If you use this as a form of punishment for something small,
what do you do after this? I control the boys by shaking their sense of

pride, by ignoring them, shaming them, making the class laugh at them, making them feel that I am angry.

Physical punishment conjures a set of complex reactions, as best articulated by an experienced teacher in a boys' school:

> I don't respect hitting as a form of punishment because I was hit often, but I don't rule it out either. I keep it as a last resort. I'm afraid of it because it nourishes the revenge instinct and it provides an outlet for rage and could get out of hand.

On Knowledge

When it comes to the curriculum, teachers have little flexibility and are obliged to teach the official textbooks which they describe as "uninspiring," "of low quality," and "not interesting." How, then, is a teacher to deal with a textbook with which he or she has an adversarial relationship? A number of teachers specifically made reference to the importance of stimulating dialogue as opposed to inculcation. But by "dialogue" they seem to be referring to a technique in which the teacher asks questions to students in the expectation of receiving a single, fixed, correct answer. The notion of dialogue does not seem to refer to a critical, exploratory, open-ended approach to the subject material. Given the fixed nature of the school curriculum and limited time, true dialogue is not a plausible technique.

A social studies teacher admits that the subject textbook confused him, nevertheless, he had to somehow convey its content so that he would not be a failure as a teacher. He supplements books with other materials when possible, such as maps, but beyond that he is tied to the book. He frowns on the external study guides available in the private market.[7]

The more creative teachers devise innovative methods and approaches to the material, but their efforts are often thwarted by supervisors and inspectors from the district offices. An Arabic teacher, in an attempt to help his students memorize the difficult grammar rules in a lighthearted way, put the lessons to songs. Despite the seeming success of his musical experiment, his supervisors reprimanded him on the grounds that singing rather than speaking lessons contradict the currently desirable modern educational methods, and they put an end to the practice.

Indeed, the continuous surveillance of teachers by inspectors seriously limits their autonomy in the classroom.

Teachers complain bitterly about inspectors who they claim use their authority and rank to embarrass and humiliate them. One teacher recounts his embarrassment at the hands of an inspector:

> The inspector was rude and liked to show off in front of the women teachers. He gave me meaningless instructions in front of my students about how to organize my teacher-preparation notebooks. He chided me for explaining the same lesson differently in two different classes, but what should I have done? The two classes were of very different levels and abilities.

Another teacher angrily explains:

> These follow-up committees have created a relation of enmity. These inspectors are no more than disgusting creatures coming to find mistakes, not to look at reality. They waste time and generate paperwork.... They don't care about the student's level, not even if the kid doesn't write.... They're like state intelligence agents.... Each one crushes the one beneath him, all the way down to the student.[8]

The constant interference of follow-up committees effects the micromanagement of schools. It also reflects how relations between boss and underling are based on a lack of trust. Regardless of whether or not it is possible to generalize from these negative experiences, one is forced to question whether follow-up committees benefit the education process.

Arts, Technology, and Quality of School Life

How can we assess the quality of school life? What becomes of nonacademic subjects, called "activities" (a euphemism among some for "a waste of time"), which are supposed to provide students with some sort of enrichment and broader education? The school newspaper, for example, an activity that is supposed to foster awareness and creativity, is seen by some as a tiresome burden. One female teacher explains:

> The staff responsible for the school paper would collect money and give it to a professional calligrapher to do the work. The sheet of poster paper is always the same, but the lead article, copied from somewhere, changes. It deals with one of the standard approved

themes of women's issues, famous Egyptians such as Ahmed Zewail
(Egyptian Nobel prize winner in Science, 1999), or sports.

Art and music are also largely regarded as a waste of time. "Of what
use is Music?" one teacher asks. It is perhaps the lack of adequate
resources that drives some teachers to consider the arts negatively. One
teacher pointed out that art teachers must work in "a dismal art room"
with a class of one hundred students or with broken-down musical
instruments. Instead of using their time on the nongraded subjects of
music and art, teachers prefer to use every available moment of the
school day to prepare students for their exams in the core subjects.

As for technological equipment such as overhead projectors and
computers, the teachers express a generally cynical view about them.
"These technological gadgets are meaningless," one teacher argues. "You
get an overhead projector in order to say 'I have the most advanced
equipment,' yet the teacher hasn't been trained to use it. And color
prints, of what use are they?" A single machine was available for up to
sixty students at a time, but, as one teacher points out, "they're not
allowed to touch it, and teachers aren't well-trained in using and fixing
it. The kids just use them to watch cartoons." The computer, however,
has yielded certain indirect benefits to schools; in one case it speeded up
the introduction of electricity, and in another, led to a phone line.

The physical condition of school buildings leaves much to be
desired and affects the quality of schooling. One teacher recounts how
his school finally received electricity after waiting for years, but that it
brought new problems because the wiring is exposed and the danger of
electric shock is ever present. As a safety measure, the teachers form a
human shield around the electrical poles on rainy days until all the students leave the school, an illustration of how Egyptians show solidarity
in situations of catastrophe.

School communities are also forced to work together in a situation
of "enforced solidarity" to maintain even minimal levels of safety and
sanitation at schools. A school principal noted that his school's maintenance budget was spent in the first week. Therefore the school had to
rely on donations, usually from parents, for paints, windows, light bulbs,
and even sewage disposal. Vandalism exacerbates the issue of school
maintenance. This same school principal complains, "I bought forty
faucets and the next day didn't find them. The students removed them,
pure vandalism." One teacher asserts: "Some might say vandalism

wouldn't happen if the students felt they had even a small share of that property. And this is true." He further suggested that vandalism, including graffiti on school walls, represented a form of resistance. Egyptians mark public and private spaces with excerpts of songs, proverbs, colloquial expressions, religious invocations for God's protection, or simply the names of cherished persons. In *The Clamor of the Silent* (1971), the sociologist Sayed Eweiss studies those "visible transcripts" as forms of resistance. Does what is written on the walls of Egyptian schools then constitute "a clamor of the silent"?

Political Cultures of Teachers

If we consider education as a profession, then why are teachers not afforded the professionalism of those in medicine, law, and engineering? Teachers are, without a doubt, more numerous than other professional groups, but neither abundance nor courage has won the day as the huge body of teachers remains dormant, disconnected, and lacking in professional organization. The Teachers' Union (*Niqabat al-Mualimeen*) was founded in 1954, but does not seem to have been relevant to the professional lives of teachers. It represents a membership, a pension, and, at most, a social or recreational club. One teacher recounts, "Teachers are marginalized on purpose. If the syndicate was free the teacher would be free. Teachers do not have a position as a social group, nor do they have a sense of themselves as a [professional] group." One young teacher describes how he tried to participate in his union's elections, only to encounter one impediment after another. He arrived at his own branch office to cast his ballot and found neither a polling committee nor a ballot box. Those elected were, according to his estimation, opportunistic people working in an atmosphere where corruption prevailed and who simply wanted to make use of perks such as discount vacation spots that came with the office.

The same primary school teacher told me about his experience at an official demonstration in which his colleagues participated begrudgingly and under the threat that their absence would be reported: "But they came back from the demonstration rejuvenated. It was the first time they expressed their opinion. Primary school teachers do not have the experience of university [with its student politics]." He also recalled a rare moment of camaraderie between the teachers when the school's satellite dish was switched from the usual educational channels to Al-Jazeera news during the second Gulf War. He was astonished that his colleagues were so receptive to hearing a discourse different in tone from that of official state media.

The general lack of collective action among teachers is compounded by a lack of solidarity brought about by competition and hierarchy within the profession. As one teacher states, "the opportunity for one teacher depends on the abolition of the other." Similarly, factionalism and favors based on primordial ties prevails among teachers. One teacher points out, "If a school's deputy is from the village of Ayat, the next thing you know the entire school faculty is from Ayat." Another teacher told how a gang of teachers from the same region controlled a school in an industrial neighborhood to the extent that they actually drove away principals not to their liking. They also ran the private lesson activities and used the school as their meeting place for eating and smoking water pipes after school hours.

The Market of Private Lessons

I pause here at an emphatic comment made by a secondary school history teacher in reference to the vast private lesson market: "With the material goal, the teacher loses his dignity; profit-making diminishes status." Teachers tend to differentiate between acceptable and unacceptable ways of giving private lessons. According to a former school principle, it is usually acceptable for teachers to give private lessons at the request of parents in private homes, however it is not dignified for them to work with the private lesson centers, or as part of the lesson mafias. The use of the term "mafia" corresponds to popular vocabulary that has evolved around the sometimes shady activity of private lessons. The term "head" represents the student, an "injection" a lesson, and the paying customer is described as either "cold," "comfortable," or "befeathered," based on the standard of his home.

The potential for corruption and problems associated with private lessons is great. Sometimes members of school administrations collude to raise prices above advertised ones and to increase the number of students per study group to maximize their profits. Private teachers also sometimes become too familiar with their students' families leading one to wonder if this sort of relationship is in the interest of the student. One teacher pointed to an especially problematic area of teacher-parent relations, "the teacher's relation to the student's mother." Male teachers may be accused, particularly by neighbors, of having inappropriate relations with students' mothers. One teacher relates that when a mother found out her son failed the year despite taking private lessons she screamed, "All the money we paid; we fed him, I slept with him ... the boy fails ... how come!?"

Teachers also lose legitimacy and respect when they peddle their services to parents in a crass commercial manner, as one teacher explains:

> Part of the teacher's image is tied to the way he markets lessons: he sits in the school before classes start ready to pounce upon the parent. 'Forget about Mr. So and So, I will give a lesson for such and such an amount.' Negotiations are like the bargaining that takes place in the vegetable market. Teachers try to justify private lessons and make them seem *halal* (Islamically acceptable) by arguing, 'No one is forced to take them, and you still do your share in the classroom.' Realistically, it doesn't make sense. If you did your part in the classroom the student wouldn't need the private lesson.

Yet not all private lessons exchanges are shrouded in corruption. Some teachers lower their fees for students of modest means to provide them with an equal chance as students from more affluent families. All the teachers were careful to distance themselves from the negative stereotype of teachers scurrying "from house, to school, to lessons."

Taken together, these scenarios clarify the discrepancy between the importance of the wager and the actors, and the distinction between the profession and the vocation. It ought to be stressed that this wager/actor dichotomy can be applied in other realms, such as health care, notwithstanding the distance separating the highly-elevated profession of medicine from that of teaching. It is not a coincidence that we find a comparable problem in education and medicine since they are both spheres that are intimately related to the humanity of human beings and to their rights in modern society. In education, the institutional expressions always remain lower than the level of the wager, which explains why education in Egypt and in other societies is always in a state of reformation. Hence, by definition, we are facing a problem that cannot be totally solved, and which seems to be getting increasingly problematic. I think this is what one teacher who loves the profession means when he says: "As a teacher, I wish I was from the previous generation. . . . The ten years make a difference."

Interactions

My intention in the previous pages has been to describe interactions that took place between the researcher and the subjects, namely the teachers, in light of the current climate in which they are so often held up as scapegoats for a range of social ills. Generally speaking, interviews have a special significance because they can enable us to adopt and make use of the subjects' language and unique expressions to reformulate public discourse.

There was, without question, a desire on the part of the teachers to talk, to have their voices and testimonies heard. Some of them stressed certain "recommendations"—as in the ritual closing sessions of academic symposia—while others held to the idea that the researcher, even if not holding an official government position, should at least in one way or another be connected to a project (and how numerous they are) for educational reform, for, if not, "then what use is the research?" And so they made the researcher bear the responsibility of making their voices heard by officials. Indeed, officials were the ever present ghosts during interviews, whether in the form of adversaries or overseers.

This leads to questions about the sensitivity of conducting this type of research, and the fears teachers express about being under surveillance by their superiors. In spite of stressing that personal information would not be revealed (and that it was, in any case, unimportant to the researcher), some of the teachers deliberately resorted to ambiguity to conceal their identities. This type of fear leads one to conclude that if the education apparatus serves as the main tool of political and social control to which all Egyptian students theoretically submit, then this control is also practiced and internalized by its trustees and main actors, namely the teachers.

If protecting the identity of research subjects is an obvious aspect of the ethics of the research profession, there is another type of protection that is difficult to achieve, namely the protection of the subjects' words from misinterpretation and misquoting, whether in terms of the researcher's writing and the selectivity of her listening, or in terms of what the reader gleans from the text. The researcher hopes to return the goods, the words and experiences of teachers, to their rightful owners; in other words, to provoke reactions and comments by teachers, starting with those who participated in the game.

The opinions and views that the teachers divulged to the researcher might not differ substantially from the prevalent public discourse—

whether journalistic or academic—about education. Thus, it is not certain to what extent teachers separated their actual practices and opinions from official discourse about what those should be. There is also a form of critical discourse within the official educational establishment itself, the purpose of which sometimes seems to preempt outside criticism in such a way that the necessity of reform appears as a national and technical mission which all parties in the social game agree upon, as if they were all equal. The concept of the rulers' political responsibility remains far from the discourse. All these concerns were present in the interviews and had an epistemological impact on the researcher and researched subjects alike.

My intention, therefore, is not to delve into the reality of the practices, but rather, to look at teachers' expressions of this reality, and the ways in which they bestow meaning on their practices. Another objective of this work has been to chart the stages and important landmarks of the professional path, including the memory of decisive situations and moments, the ways of resolving or overcoming conflicts, the areas where work-related worries overlap with those of daily life, and the methods employed to harmonize, resolve, or transcend possible contradictions and tensions. Such tensions include those between the official job and profit-making, between the exaggerated appreciation of the teacher's vocation and the social decline of his/her status, and between the classroom as a space where the teacher holds center stage as the main creative actor while administrative restrictions impose low-risk acts and practices that lead to a loss of the teacher's autonomy. As for the final, perhaps more optimistic point, the completion of this text, of any text, is only fulfilled in its reading. The previous pages will only acquire their meaning when read by the people most concerned: the teachers; the teachers of today and the teachers of the future.

Notes to Chapter 4

1. Teacher training institutes were derogatorily referred to as "the Citadel of Dunlop and the Trojan Horse of the occupation." Douglas Dunlop, Advisor to the Ministry of Education (1906–1909) represents a figure of evil in Egyptian historiography. According to the dominant narrative, he did everything he could to limit the education of Egyptians and to impose the English language on them in order to perpetuate British colonial domination. The goal

of education was to produce the necessary civil servants for the state bureaucracy. Until now, Dunlop is present in contemporary debates about national sovereignty versus foreign expertise or interventions.

It appears here as though Lewis Awad is reviving old disputes between Taha Hussein (1889–1973) and Ismail El-Qabbani (1898–1954), or between Sayed Qutb (1906–1966) and Ismail El-Qabbani. Qabbani, Minister of Education between 1952–1954 and founding father of modern pedagogy, came to be the common enemy of enlightened prominent intellectuals like Taha Hussein (Minister of Education 1950–1952), as well as radical social thinkers like Sayed Qutb, even before the later turned to Islamic radicalism. It is ironic that calls to reconsider the educational formation of teachers were made twice: in the 1960s as part of an Anglo-Americanization movement, and in the 1990s as part of a clearly political call to curb the spread of Islamist trends in education colleges.

2. A few months later, in April 1999, students of the Faculty of Education of Ayn Shams University (east of Cairo) demonstrated against what they perceived as state betrayal. Several students were arrested and then released. According to officials the disturbances were due to a few agitators.

3. Here, I would like to thank my research "subject": Mrs. Gawdat, Mohamed, Ahmed, Adel, Omar, Ramadan and Magdy, and Ms. Amina for all the time they gave me.

4. The researcher found the subjects of this research through personal contacts and the interviews took place in public places or in the homes of the researched subjects, far from the context of work or the school atmosphere. I relied on taking notes, rather than on tape-recording and each interview took between two to three hours. This group gave generously of their time, time taken from their periods of rest, leisure, gaining a livelihood, and the concerns of daily life, so that they could talk about teaching and teachers, a topic full of woes, with a researcher whom, with one exception, they did not know. Among them are graduates of the Faculty of Arts, Dar Al-Ulum, and education colleges and institutes. Five teachers and one former principal work at public-sector schools, one is a teacher at a private school, and one is a teacher in a technical secondary school. The teachers' specializations are Arabic, English, history, social studies, and philosophy.

5. Wafd was the leading nationalist and most popular party between 1920 and 1950. Mutanabbi is a famous Arab poet.

6. Using a qualitative, open-ended mode of interviewing, an unusual research method in Egypt where the questionnaire is so widespread, the researcher had to persuade the subjects of the validity of this approach. From

the start, the researcher did not resort to anything remotely like a police interrogation, did not try to make the subjects speak against their will, or cast doubt on what they said. Rather, the researcher's role was confined to listening and posing questions, sharing experiences when possible, and putting forward her opinions, assumptions, and impressions about the subjects, in addition to stressing, from the beginning, her unshakeable ethical commitment to guaranteeing their anonymity.

7. Due to the poor quality of textbooks, a large private market provides external study guides. These guides are intended to help the student prepare for exams and provide sets of questions and answers, exercises, previous exams, and summaries of the lessons. The idea is to aid the student to memorize as much as possible with the fewest words and efforts.

8. The teacher also noted how inspectors are especially tuned in to the nationally instated school projects of the day which include: cleanliness, the network connections with the Ministry under the so-called "e-government" project, and the productive school (selling of small products, especially food, to raise revenues which are shared between schools and the Ministry).

References

Awad, Lewis. 1964. *Al-Jama'a wa'l-Mujtama' Al-Jadeed* [The University and the New Society] Cairo: Dirassat Ishtirakiya.

Aroyan, Loïs. 1983. *The Nationalization of Arabic and Islamic Education in Egypt: Dar al-Ulum and al-Azhar.* Cairo: *Cairo Papers in Social Science.*

Castel, Robert. 1995. *Les Métamorphoses de la Question Sociale, une Chronique du Salariat.* Paris: Fayard.

El-Hakei, Ali Hassan. 1938. *Mushkilat Al-Tarbeyya fi Misr* [The Problems of Education in Egypt]. Cairo: Maktabat al-Kashif.

El-Asaad, Mohamed Abu. 1993. "Tatawwur Niqabat Al-Mu'allemeen Al-Misreyyin" [The Development of the Egyptian Teachers' Sydicate]. Cairo: Al-Hay'a Al-Misriyya Al-'Amma l'il-Kitab, p.59.

Eweiss, Sayed. 1971. *Hutaf al-Samitin, Zahirat al-kitaba 'ala hayakil al-markabat fil-mujtama' al-misri al-mu'asir* [The Clamor of the Silent: Inscriptions in Modern Egyptian Society]. Cairo: Dar al-Tiba'a al-haditha.

Farag, Iman. 1999. *La Construction Sociale D'une Education Nationale; Enjeux Politiques Et Trajectoires Educatives, Egypte Première Moitié Du Xxe Siècle.* Thèse de doctorat, Paris: EHESS.

5

What are Teachers Transmitting? Pedagogic Culture in Rural Egypt

FADIA MAUGITH

Summary

In poor rural areas where illiteracy is high, teachers may be the only educated adult role models with whom children interact on a regular basis. As such, teachers hold the potential of providing children with the tools and necessary means for social and cultural improvement. The main question guiding this research is, therefore, what is the culture of the teacher in rural schools and what is he/she transmitting to students by way of tastes, values, attitudes, and behaviors? Through ten vignettes, derived from case studies of rural schoolteachers, this research presents a range of teachers' attitudes and practices. The findings indicate the prevalence of a culture of submission, patriarchy, and extremism, however one in which alternatives exist and where change can be possible.

Rural Teachers as Agents of Cultural Transmission

Much of rural Egypt suffers from acute levels of poverty, underdevelopment, illiteracy, and a growing cultural conservatism. Teachers may be the only educated adult role models with whom children interact on a regular basis. As such, teachers hold the potential of providing children with the tools and necessary means for social and cultural improvement.

Along these lines, the main question guiding this research is: what is the culture of the teacher in the rural school and what is she transmitting to students by way of tastes, values, attitudes, and behavior? This topic holds a special interest for the researcher who, while currently a resident of Cairo, grew up in a rural community as the daughter of a school teacher. Always in the back of my mind as I conducted this research was the reference of my broad-minded father and his rural colleagues from the 1950s and 1960s, who pushed for girls' education and equality, treated Muslim and Christian students on equal grounds, practiced a form of Islam that encouraged openness, curiosity, and commitment to excellence, and provided quality education for the poor. Part of my motivation in carrying out this study was to try to understand the current culture of education in rural Egypt, which is regrettably different from what I had experienced as a child and youth.

The fieldwork for this study was conducted with teachers from a group of schools in three small villages in the Egyptian Delta. While this study began as a study on the general culture of schooling, it evolved into case studies of ten teachers with special emphasis on their cultural attitudes. Presented as ten vignettes, this research is based on the understanding that an awareness of the teacher's cultural make-up can allow us to probe critical questions relating to how the teacher might be capable of being a tool for cultural change and not just for curriculum transmission. It can be said that among all the elements that make up education—it is the curricula, the administration, extracurricular activities, peers, teaching methods and aids, buildings and facilities—it is the teacher, with his/her behavior and example, who bears the most important influence on a child's schooling. It is through the teacher that educational plans and ideas come to life. Especially in the classroom, teachers play a most prominent role in reinforcing and reproducing society's values, behavioral patterns, cognitive skills, and culture (Gage 1978). The teacher's influence, therefore, is especially important during the compulsory basic education stage of schooling (grades 1–8).

This research is guided by methodological principles of critical ethnography, which deals with cultural processes (Spindler 1997, 26–27). Critical and interpretative ethnography is a necessary means of discovering the forces at work in cultural production, and provides clarity for understanding actual conditions and practices of schooling. One of the most essential tools of this methodology is direct observation and interaction, both of which require the researcher to possess a high level of conversational and communication skills, and an ability to delve into the depths of events and ideas. The researcher should also be cognizant of the rules that regulate the education system, be familiar with the conditions that teachers work in, possess knowledge about pedagogic norms and possibilities, and have an awareness of the set of relations and regulations that guide classroom interactions.

I realized early on that teachers are not accustomed to the ethnographic method. They regard fixed questionnaires and formal evaluations as legitimate forms of knowledge gathering. I did, in fact, distribute a questionnaire to one hundred respondents in order to gauge some basic cultural and political attitudes. These questions, which were followed-up by one-on-one interviews and classroom observations, deal with teacher attitudes towards democracy, women and gender equity, attitudes about peace with Israel,[1] and the role of the school in fostering dialogue and tolerance. The questionnaire served as a starting point, and also as a way for me to introduce myself into the school communities. The difficulties came about later when I kept returning to the schools, long after the questionnaire had been filled, to engage teachers in further discussions. It required much effort on my part to deal with the teachers' skepticism towards the ethnographic method. To avoid the kind of formulaic, stock answers that teachers were used to giving in quantitative research, I conducted interviews in a more informal, chatty manner. Recording and note-taking during these meetings were not easy tasks as respondents were initially uncomfortable with their opinions being recorded, and worried that I might report the contents of our talks to some higher authorities. It took some time to convince them that their identities would be concealed and that I was a genuine academic researcher. Gradually the teachers became more relaxed with the method.

For the record, I would like to state that a spirit of goodwill and cooperation existed between members of the local district education office, school principals, deputies, and teachers during the course of this study. The school community welcomed me warmly throughout the entire four month research period in 2003. At first I attributed this warm reception to the legendary hospitality of Egyptian rural society. But it became clear that the community was eager to participate because they regarded it as a way to reach education officials. There was an overwhelming desire on the part of most participants to work towards improving both the education system and the conditions under which they worked. By sharing aspects of their work and lives with me, these teachers, even those whose words ring with hostility and anger, hoped that their participation would lead to a greater awareness of their struggles and situations. The female teachers who cooperated with me were seriously interested in benefiting from the experience. They asked me many questions about how to provide their daughters with a future that will ensure the rights to which they are entitled. For my part, my hope is to provide portraits, variously hopeful, distressing, and complex, of the driving issues pertinent to the struggle for critical pedagogy in rural Egypt.

Vignettes on Education and Culture

The ten teachers profiled in this study were chosen according to a general set of criteria. An attempt was made to select teachers with a range of attitudes on the issues raised in the questionnaire. Some consideration was also made to gender and religious diversity; of the ten cases, seven teachers are male, three female, and one Christian. As a guiding interest of this research is the transmission of culture, teachers who specialized in subjects related to elements of artistic, literary, and local culture were selected for this study. The sample, therefore, includes teachers of theatre, culture (*thaqafa*), library (a subject responsible for conveying principles of reading and research), school broadcasting, Arabic (because of its association with literary and religious culture), English (with its emphasis on literature and global culture), physical education, music, and agriculture (which serves as a subject that reinforces local culture). It is important to keep in mind that teachers are undoubtedly subject to difficult symbolic and material conditions that curb their performance. An overwhelming majority of teachers boldly and clearly stated that the conditions of their profession are unacceptable. They wish for improved educational facilities, for signs of appreciation, for the kind of support that would enable them to employ their creative energies, and for fair and livable wages.

Case Study # 1: Tolerant Conservatism

A male theater teacher of twenty-four claims to spend all his extra time reading the Quran. His mission appears to be to convert all Muslim acquaintances to his way of conservative religious thinking. Despite my being of the generation of his mother, he expressed his disapproval that I did not wear an Islamic headscarf, and took it upon himself to preach to me on the Muslim dress code for women. In response to my *"sabah al-kheir"* (good morning) he replied with the religious Islamic salutation: *as-salamu aleykm wa rahmat allahu wa barakatu* (Peace be unto you and God's mercy and blessings). It was clear that he was someone who insisted on his own way of thinking.

He believes that instead of culture, people should spend their time only in pursuit of sciences, or more specifically, the divine sciences. He experimented with reading nonreligious texts when he was at university, but found they all led him astray from the Righteous Path. His discourse was filled with scorn towards intellectuals and writers, and he made statements such as, "all journalists are buffoons and are either agents of the state or agents of the West, especially the secularists ones." He always talked as if he was the only one who was right.

In response to my question about gender equality he notes:

> women [like you] come along and give us headaches with your foreign talk about women's liberty. This is nonsense. It's a foreign conspiracy against us because the West does not want us to undergo the real renaissance present in Islam, and that is why they fight Islam.

He asserts that the most important quality of his future wife would be her knowledge of the limits assigned her by God and her husband. For only such a woman, he explains, could work without causing any fear [of immoral behavior outside the home].

Despite his claims to not accept views opposing his own, he is surprisingly tolerant in the classroom. He shows tolerance to his students and does not subject them to physical or psychological punishment, as was a norm at his school. He allows students to ask questions at the end of a lecture and always answers them calmly and patiently. Students appear to genuinely like him and to listen to him with interest. Despite his stated conservative views, his classroom provides the space for some degree of dialogue.

Case Study # 2: Theater without Plays

A second theater teacher, a young man of twenty-four, has not read any plays or drama criticism since he graduated from the Faculty of

Specific Education (which includes specialization in the nonfoundational subjects such as theater, home economics, art, and music). He asserts that the only book he needs is the Quran.

During his lessons, he departs from the curriculum only to expound on his vision for an Islamic state. "The Muslim government is imminent, Allah willing, and with it everything in society will change, everything deviating from divine law (*sharia*) will be punished according to Islamic law and not according to the laws of the imperialist West." He later adds: "Why espouse [a Western-style] democracy when we have a clear text, the *shura* [for Islamic democracy]?" He believes the greatest period in Arab history is the early Abbasid and Ommayed dynasties—and not because of their scientific achievement and intellectual openness as I expected, but because its rulers "feared God and ruled according to the Quran."

He is the supervisor of the extracurricular speech society, a group without any female student members. The only reason he does not punish students physically is because the Minister punishes teachers who do, a situation that, according to him, has led to the deterioration of pupils' manners and behavior. He talks often about Islam and uses religion to support all his views. He trivializes any other point of view and accuses those who disagreed with him of being ignorant.

Case Study # 3: Physical Education without Girls

This physical education teacher in a coeducational primary school loves sports, but does not like to teach. He aspired to play professional football, but when that didn't work out, he resorted to teaching. He is carefree and lighthearted with the kids. The boys seem to like him in spite of his occasional use of excessive physical punishment. I became close to this teacher, relying on the fact that we have something in common: I have a BA in physical education (PE).

While observing his classes, I noticed two disturbing phenomena. Although PE is a required subject for all students, the teacher excludes girls from the class. Sometimes the girls are simply nowhere to be seen during the PE class; at other times, they sit in a row on the ground with their backs to the wall, cross-legged, hands folded in their laps, to clear the way for the boys to play. When asked why girls are not involved in the class, the teacher answers that girls by nature do not like sports and prefer to study. He also claims that he is simply protecting the girls because the boys could bump into them and knock them over. He finally adds that what the school curricula and education supervisors stipulate is one thing, but what is proper in village society is quite another: it simply would not do for girls to jump up and down, bodies shaking, in front of boys. The second disturbing aspect is this teacher's indifference and violence. On a morning when I was observing his class, he gave the football to the male students to start a game of soccer and with his whistle delegated a boy as the referee. After a few minutes a fight broke out between the two teams, evidently because the boys objected to a call of the referee. The teacher fell upon them, hitting and punching them on their bodies and faces without distinction. On another day, a parent came to the playground with his son who had gotten into a fight the previous day and had sustained a bleeding wound in the area around the eye. The teacher witnessed the fight but showed no concern for the injured boy and neither sent him to the hospital, nor to his home. The boy's father threatened to report the matter to the police and to sue the school if his son's eye was damaged. Is this an environment that can foster team play, group responsibility, physical skill, and health?

Case Study #4: A Music Teacher Confronts Conservatism

The twenty-seven-year-old music teacher has a cheerful and optimistic disposition. He loves all forms of art and plans to retire from teaching when it becomes possible for him to live off of his income as a professional accordion player. He prefers teaching girls to boys and spends time giving his fifteen-year-old sister singing lessons to help her get into a musical institute. Unlike many of his colleagues, who consider singing a disreputable career for women, he has no objections to his sister becoming a professional singer. He speaks sarcastically about his colleagues' criticisms of art and music.

He believes, without the slightest reservation, that women should be equal to men, and claims that they are sometimes superior to them. He would not be able to play music well, he explains, unless women would also have that opportunity. He asserts that women possess beautiful feelings and dispositions and the capacity to love, whereas men, "as you can see [in reference to his conservative colleagues], are only capable of spite and censure and the disfigurement of all that is beautiful. My hands that play the most beautiful of tunes are incapable of hitting a human or even an animal."

He posits that Egyptian schools are full of talents and beautiful voices, but they are lacking in means and musical equipment. His monthly teaching salary is equal to one night's work playing a wedding party. He has aspirations to organize a school music and song concert, but considers it a far-fetched dream because he lacks means, and also because of expected opposition from some colleagues, who would see it as silly rubbish, that is to say, as a sign of "moral laxity," and others who would see it as a sign of "religious unbelief."

Case Study # 5: Mixing Fear with Respect

"Saeed," a 40-year-old broadcasting teacher, is responsible for developing the writing and reporting skills of students in grades six to eight. He limits his own reading to interpretations of the Quran (*tafsir*), which he reads constantly, and occasionally the daily semioffi-cial newspaper, *Al-Ahram*. He never wanted to be a teacher, but an army officer, and he employs semimilitary tactics in the classroom. When displeased with students, he would scold them in a cruel lan-guage and accuse them of being stupid and ignorant. He often physi-cally punishes both male and female students, a treatment, he told me, which he extends to his own children and sometimes his wife. He considers the students' fear to be proof of their respect for him. He lectures straight out of the textbook, discourages students from asking questions, and deviates from the lesson only to expound on his own life, which he does frequently.

In his opinion, the educational, economic, and political problems of Egyptian society are the result of society's straying from divine law (*sharia*). When asked if he thinks women should have liberty on par with men he responds: "This is all errant talk; the word 'liberty' is inappropriate for a Muslim woman.... As for equality with men, she is not fit for that either." With four children to support, he does not know how to make ends meet and is unable to fulfill all their mater-ial wants.

The students are always happy to hear the bell signaling the end of his class. Is this an environment where writing and communication tal-ents can really be developed?

Case Study # 6: The Bureaucratization of a Teacher

A forty-three-year-old male vice principle and culture teacher complains of having been turned from an educator to a bureaucrat. "I spend two hours a day writing reports about the school's activities, even though there are no means available for such activities. The Ministry does not want real education," he complains. "It keeps us distracted with slogans like, 'My School Is Beautiful and Clean,' not to forget the 'Productive School.'"

He chose teaching out of conviction of its importance, but has been disappointed by the profession. "The truly excellent teacher isn't appreciated or rewarded by material or non-material means" he complains. "The excellent ones are on equal footing with the negligent ones in this country, and things are getting worse." He is frustrated by not being able to direct and control teachers' performance or to provide them with incentives to improve because the Ministry has essentially stripped administrators of any power. He recounts that if a teacher hits a student his punishment is three months behind bars, but if he hits a principal or vice principal, his punishment is only three days. So, he asks, "who should the teacher hit?"

He likes and sometimes composes poetry. His happiest moments are when he is giving his brother, a farmer, a hand on the land. He would like both of his daughters to become doctors. His wife is an employee at the village bank. He sometimes helps her with the housework, but does not believe that women are fit to be equal with men. He does not hit the students since they are young, and jokes with them in class. His students always seem happy to see him.

Case Study # 7: On Sectarianism and Tolerance

The agriculture teacher is a man of forty-two and one of the few Christian teachers in the school. I asked him if the fact that he is Christian has an effect on his relations with colleagues. He says his relations are okay except that he sometimes feels they treat him unfairly [because he's Christian]. Although he enjoys teaching, he often dislikes the teaching profession, especially when he's confronted with misinformation and ignorance regarding Christians. He relates, "The students surprise me with their spontaneous, unchecked questions they bring from their homes. They'll stop me in class to ask, 'So and so says such and such about Christians. Is it true?'...The situation has gotten much worse in the last five years."

I asked him if he sometimes feels unity with Muslims, such as at the festival of the saint Deir Al-Malak's birthday (*moulid*), at the village of Bai al-Arab in which both Muslims and Christians celebrate. He laments that while that might have been the case in the past, the situation has changed: "My mother tells me about this celebration when she was young and I wish I had lived during those times. Now, for the past thirty years, we're afraid of everything. Half of my family has emigrated."

He has a plot of land on which he plants flowers that are sold in Cairo. "I make twice as much from these flowers than I do from my teaching salary," he notes, but he enjoys teaching and passing on his knowledge of agriculture to the students. He feels that low salaries lead many teachers to take their responsibilities lightly and also cause the children to take school lightly. It upsets him to hears his students—who are themselves from peasant families—say that they only take his class because it's an easy subject.

Girls are a rarity in his classes and he believes they do not like the subject. With regard to his own daughters, he would very much like to see them complete their education and to work, an attitude he doesn't hold for his wife. "My wife," he notes somewhat jokingly, "no, she shouldn't work, and that's that!"

He claims to have no time for reading and says he knows nothing about politics, however he does say that he supports peace with Israel. He is afraid of expressing this opinion publicly since some of his colleagues would consider such a stance tantamount to treason.

He is gentle with his students and never uses physical or psychological punishment with them. Perhaps because of his position as a minority, he is the only one who wrote about tolerance in the questionnaire with the comment, "there should be love and peace between Christians and Muslims because they are the sons of one nation. Religion is for God, and the nation is for all."

Case Study #8: An Unwitting English Teacher

This thirty-three-year-old English teacher received her undergraduate degree in history and education, yet she can barely talk about major events in Egypt's recent history such as the reasons for the 1973 October War. She became an English teacher by default. She regrets entering the teaching profession even though it was initially her choice to enter an education college, albeit to please a male relative—her future husband—who wanted her to teach because, in his view, it was the "only workplace suitable for women." Her husband wants their daughters to pursue more prestigious careers and aim for being a doctor and an engineer. For her part, she doesn't think women are fit for equality with men. When I pressed her to explain why, she didn't have her own ideas on the matter, but said: "Could everyone around us be wrong?" I sensed she had a strong desire to amend her ideas, but lacked the tools to do so.

She did not hide the fact that her English skills are substandard and that she has no interest in reading in her spare time, but only in watching the television serials. During a class she spelled the word "ball" incorrectly on the blackboard and when I questioned her about it after class, she laughed and said:

> The students also don't know how to spell it, neither do their parents, and at the end of the school year I pass them all. I don't have a bad professional conscience. After all, the kids who will go on to higher levels of study don't rely on the school for learning. The families that want their kids to learn make sure they get private tuition. And the specialized teacher will give them the correct information.

She spends a lot of time in class joking around, and is not bothered if quarrels broke out between her pupils.

In addition to her work as a teacher, she also performs all the housework, oversees her children's homework, and helps her husband's family with farming their land. Her husband pressured her to quit her job because, being a math teacher, he earns a sufficient supplementary income from giving private lessons, but so far she has resisted. Because she has no time at home, she prepares the next day's lesson plan hurriedly during her classes. She doesn't want her daughters to turn out like her: exhausted and incapable of changing the mode of her life.

Case Study #9: A Librarian Who Doesn't Read

The thirty-six-year-old librarian laughs when I asked her about what she reads in her free time. "I don't like to read," she comments. "I don't have reading material and I also don't have time to read." Most of the library's paltry holdings consist of donations from schoolteachers and are mainly religious in nature. They include leaflets on the veil, marriage in Islam, the Muslim prayer for travel, the prayer for sleep, and other religious pamphlets.

She's been divorced and remarried and speaks with great bitterness about how she suffers from the cruelty shown divorced women by village folk. Following her divorce she became prey for male colleagues, and married female colleagues avoided her. Her situation drove her to accept the first marriage proposal she received. Her second husband, a government employee, earns only a modest salary, so she takes full financial responsibility for her son from her first marriage. Her ex-husband did not want her to remarry, despite having remarried and fathered two children with his new wife, and he refuses to provide financial support for his son.

In her opinion, a woman needs to have a man upon whom she can depend: a brother, father, or even a son. She believes that democracy is a subject that does not concern women for it is men who vote [legally women are allowed to vote], are elected [some women hold public office], and talk about politics. "Why," she asks, "should I exhaust myself trying to understand something that is of no use to me?" She considers herself unlucky and does not expect to be happy one day because, as she put it, once unlucky, always unlucky.

Case Study #10: An Arabic Teacher Who Dislikes Language

This young women of twenty-one years, is an Arabic teacher who dislikes Arabic grammar and only entered the Arabic language department at university "because we were a group of school friends who wanted to stay together." She shows no interest in reading and seems unaware of the wealth of Arabic periodicals and literature. Her students, whom she regularly pinches since hitting is forbidden, show signs of fear of her.

She aspires to get married to a colleague who works as a primary school teacher. He lacks the means to provide for her and formally ask for her hand in marriage. She feels it's unfair that a girl's parents tend to disapprove of the love choice of their daughter, but not that of a son. She recounts that as soon as her brother fell in love, "everyone was in support of my brother, asking my father to go and meet the girl's family and ask for her hand. There will never be equality between women and men in the village like you have in Cairo, not even in a million years." She herself wants to eventually move to Cairo because of the greater possibilities there for giving private lessons. She explains:

> ...private lessons in the city can bring in a good income, unlike in the village where people don't take that many private lessons, and sometimes expect them as favors. Anyway, the study groups only net LE 5.60 per head per month. Money is the most important thing in life now because it provides good health, better education, and respect.

To her, political awareness has always meant trouble. At university she saw how security guards harassed students who were involved in politics. She intends to prevent her future children from talking about or being interested in politics to keep them out of trouble. "But, if conditions change, why not?"

Pedagogic Culture in Rural Egypt

However brief these glimpses of teachers' attitudes and lives, they allow us some scope to interpret the school environment and pedagogic culture in rural Egypt. Each case study reveals that the individual teacher contains a contradictory set of cultural traits that, at first glance, appear as a confusing mix of fixed and shifting elements. The teachers appear to be reflecting conflicts, attitudes, and movements taking place on a larger social field, testifying how the school represents a microcosm of society. Teacher culture in these rural schools seem to be most profoundly influenced by the conservative trends, which have been growing over the past three decades. They also suffer from an overbureaucratized and underfunded work environment where pay is low, and by long-standing conservative patriarchal attitudes against gender equity.

Lifelong learning?

Government slogans of "Lifelong Learning" ring especially shallow when one considers how the educated cadres of society, the teachers, could so easily be swept away by dogmatic ideas against even the broadest acceptance of democracy and gender equity. The responses and practices of many teachers, both female and male, reveal tenaciously held attitudes about women's inequality in relation to men. The case of the P. E. teacher, who would not allow girls to participate in his class, is indicative not only of how rules are flouted at the local level and perpetuate inequality and submissiveness for girls, but also the need for further research into school practices.

Many of the teachers lacked political awareness and openness, which would motivate political participation and foster peace. For example, the question (posed in the questionnaire), of whether or not the teacher supported the idea of peace with Israel, the teachers, predictably and overwhelmingly, did not support peace. This finding was not surprising given Israel's relationship with its Arab neighbors. Although a minority of respondents cited the above reasons, the most common reason for lack of support for peace with Israel had to do with Israel's desire to demolish the Al-Aqsa Mosque [in Jerusalem] in order to rebuild Solomon's Temple. The few who did support peace with Israel, such as the agriculture teacher, were weary of stating so publicly.

Even those who support democratic ideals, such as the culture and music teachers, showed despair regarding the possibility of real democracy and reflected a heritage of fear and lack of confidence in the capacity of political institutions to respond to the power of centralized authorities. Such ideas about democracy and gender equity are not surprising if we note that several teachers exhibited deficient levels of knowledge in their own subjects and did not have the time or interest to develop their areas of expertise. The teacher education colleges were strongholds of Islamist elements in the 1980s and early 1990s and the places where these teachers may have formulated their ideas about religion, politics, and culture.

A Culture of Submission

These rural teachers, who themselves are often poor and suffering as an underclass, tend to perpetuate class relations by encouraging a culture of submission among their (poor) students. By and large, teachers regard students who are obedient, attentive, and do not question their views, as preferable. Yet it is precisely the student's cultural poverty—bred in an environment which is economically poor—that leads these student to unquestioningly accept the teacher (the authority), as the sole source of knowledge. When a student from a higher social class questions a teacher, he is seen as flouting his family's position and cultural resources.

The village teachers, therefore, subscribe to prevalent traditional standards of the good student, who is obedient and quiet, while the student who asks questions and wants constructive dialogue is considered impolite and uncouth. How can children and youths possibly learn to express individual viewpoints and ideas opposing those in positions of authority? How can they learn to practice principles of openness, acceptance, and tolerance? And when will they know it is their right to ask questions and learn how to ask these questions? Teaching that is based on problem-solving is the way to resolve contradictions that come in the way of freedom. Dialogue not only requires, but also develops, critical capabilities (Freire 1995, 60–62). Instead of dialogue, the teachers insist on more information and more facts—a quantitative notion of learning.

Conclusions: Towards a Pedagogy of Change

The most critical and difficult task ahead of us in the educational field is to work towards changing teachers' cultural attitudes and practices. As a starting point, we need to understand the contradictions and confusions in teachers' cultural orientations. It is bewildering how a teacher's stated views reflect one thing, and his behavior, another. Despite their criticisms of the system, teachers prefer to be a part of the dominant system rather than to challenge or change it. Despite constant lip service to the importance of an education that promotes critical thinking, the teacher is lacking in the intellectual and critical training and preparation that would enable him or her to express an individual viewpoint. In an atmosphere of seeming cultural sterility, there is little scope for teachers to express their own ideas and arguments. Instead, shirking confrontation, they might prefer to adapt prevalent cultural assumptions and maintain the status quo.

With regard to pedagogy, there is excessive concern with the formal dimension of teaching—as exemplified by continual inspection and the maintenance of a specified number of school days and of school day hours—at the expense of real educational quality. One of the MOE policies the teachers note as being especially absurd is the "My School is

Beautiful and Clean" slogan because, it does not correspond to reality (see Saad, chapter 3), and because of the accompanying disturbance, inspection, and submission to civil bodies that it generates. The result is that teachers and students develop a negative attitude towards this slogan. Similarly, the teachers and members of the administration find the Ministry's imposed concept of the Productive School ridiculous. How, then, can the school and the teachers therein, be capable of changing the society and of liberating the individual when teachers themselves submit to numerous restrictions and administrations are lacking in creativity and supervision? The system obstructs the spirit of creativity and curbs liberty and the means by which it is pursued (Qorany 1993, 192).

My time in the field gave me an awareness that, despite a long history in modern Egypt of liberal education, teachers are showing signs of increased withdraw into apathy, nativism, and conservatism. What are the implications of the findings for larger questions of educational reform? Change and reform cannot come about in a meaningful way until a more realistic picture of the dimensions of educational reality emerges, a prerequisite for which is the use of research methodologies that delve deeply into the culture and daily life of the school. Once we obtain a realistic picture, we can more adequately work towards formulating alternative, appropriate, and revisionist concepts of education and to restore to the teacher her elevated position so that she can lead the way in building a better society.

Note to Chapter 5

1. The question about whether Egyptians support peace with Israel, while it may initially seem as out of place in a study about pedagogy and culture, was used as a measure by the researcher to gauge the degree of political awareness and approach to political problem solving, for the Arab-Israeli conflict represents an ever present social and political preoccupation of Egyptians (editors' note).

References

Freire, Paulo. 1995. *Al-F'eil al-Thaqafi fi Sabeel al-Houriyaa* [Cultural Action for Freedom]. Trans. Ibrahim El-Kerdawi. Cairo: Markaz Al-Derassat wa'l-Ma'loumat al-Qanuniyya li Huqouq al-Insan.

Gage, Nathaniel Lees. 1978. *The scientific basis of the art of teaching*. New York: Teachers College Press.

Qorany, Ezzat. 1993. Ishkaliyyat al-Houriyya [The Problematic of Freedom]. *Aalam Al-Fikr* 22.2: 176–203.

Spindler, George. 1997. "Cultural process and ethnography: An anthropological perspective. In *Education and cultural process: anthropological approaches*, ed. George D. Spindler. Waveland Press.

6

The Colors of Change: Participation and Praxis in Egyptian Education

LINDA HERRERA

Summary

Due to a combination of factors including population pressure, scarce resources, neglect, gendered and classed attitudes, and environmental challenges, public-sector schools in Egypt experience rapid deterioration. A joint community and nongovernmental organization (NGO) initiative in an Egyptian public-sector girls' school was undertaken to explore how school facility upgrading could be achieved through a participatory action approach. This account by an action researcher provides reflections on the mutability of gender and class dynamics in school cultures; the ways in which the poor condition of a school facility negatively affects the overall education experience; and the possibilities for collaborations between students, staff, community members, the business community and NGOs. Perhaps most importantly, it illuminates how youth, by participating in decision-making on issues as basic as choosing the color to paint a classroom, can gain awareness and respect for their environment and act as catalysts for change.

Introduction: Participation and Praxis[1]

> If we not only construct more classrooms, but also zealously keep them clean, joyful, and beautiful, sooner or later the very

beauty of the space will require yet another beauty: that of com-
petence in teaching, the joy of learning, the creative imagination, with the freedom to exercise itself, the adventure of
creating.

—Paulo Freire, *Pedagogy of the City* (cited in Gadotti)

A public-sector preparatory school for girls (grades 6–8) loomed
large and bulky along a main street of a residential area in southern
Cairo. The neglected exterior of the school with its broken windows,
charred wall from a fire five years ago, and garbage piled along its outer
wall, stood in stark contrast to the tidy shops and tree-lined streets
nearby. A group of three neighbors (including the author), associated
with the international NGO the Population Council, wondered about
the effect such a rundown, physical environment might have on the
schoolgirls and teachers who worked within the school's walls.[2]
Motivated by the possibilities of combining school upgrading with participatory action, we contacted the Ministry of Education (MOE), local
educational governorate, school community, and members of the business sector and, on a volunteer basis, undertook a small upgrading initiative with the school.

The intention of this paper is not to provide a best practice model
for school upgrading that might go to scale. It is, far more humbly, an
attempt to document some key aspects of a school upgrading project
that took place over a two year period in order to understand how participatory approaches might look in a centralized education system that is
attempting to provide new spaces for community involvement. On
another note, it is a reflection on how changes of perception, practice,
and attitudes within a school community come about. The attempt to
identify moments of change relates to an interest in praxis, or thinking
and reflecting on the world in order to change it (Freire 1970), and
about the spaces that might be created in schools for youth to participate
in decision-making and action on their world, even when it has to do
with something as seemingly simple as which color to paint their classroom walls.

School facility upgrading and maintenance have been especially
pressing issues in Egypt where factors ranging from population growth,
massive urbanization, insufficient financial resources, policy neglect, and
natural disasters, have contributed to the problem of degenerating school

facilities. In 1999, the collapse of a wall at a primary school in Cairo that killed four children and injured nineteen, brought the issue of decaying schools to the national fore.[3] The MOE has since earmarked additional funds for school maintenance and welcomed partnerships with local and international NGOs, neighborhood communities, and parents to redress the needs of school maintenance and upgrading.[4]

While in the past, parents, community members, and NGOs have been allowed only limited involvement in public schools, in recent years, there has been an attempt to open up the public education system and allow greater participation. Regardless of how limited such an opening may be in practice, it has provided some new spaces for partnerships. Ministerial Decree Number 5 of 1993, and Number 464 of 1998 (Regarding Parents' and Teachers' Councils), allow parents to monitor educational quality, to make donations of money or equipment to schools, and to manage aspects of the educational process to ensure "a democratic climate inside schools" (National Centre for Educational Research and Development (NCERD) 2001, 20). In addition to the new decrees, the Council of Trustees was established to oversee parental initiatives in schools.

On another front, both local and international NGOs have been playing larger roles in trying to orient the education system towards greater participatory and child-centered approaches.[5] Participatory approaches in education, because they ideally involve the local community in identifying problems and working towards solutions, are more likely to be sustainable. In an effort to provide NGOs with support and guidelines for school-based initiatives, in 1998 the MOE established the Department for Non-governmental Educational Projects (NCERD 2001, 21).

A girls' preparatory school seemed a particularly fitting venue for a participatory action project, in part because of its inherent gender dimensions. Within the past three decades the issue of gender equity has emerged as a pivotal concern of national and international education development planners. Educational policies aimed at gender equity have included heightened educational access for girls, teacher training in gender sensitivity, curriculum development which avoids negative gender stereotyping, and support services for disadvantaged girls. Other strategies stress the importance of girls being provided with vocational training, management, and leadership skills (Stromquist 1997, 206–207).[6]

What better than a girls' preparatory school to undertake a project on participatory school upgrading?

Overused and Under Stress: The Case of a Double-shift School

Shortly after Egypt's 1952 Free Officer's Coup, also referred to as the "Socialist Revolution," scores of luxury residences belonging to aristocrats, industrialists, and colonialists were seized and converted into state schools. One such home, an elegant turn-of-the century villa originally inhabited by a princess, was sequestered and turned into a finishing school for girls. In the early 1970s, it underwent yet another transformation when it became a girls' general preparatory school. Several modifications were made on the building to accommodate its new residents: the ornate crystal chandeliers were removed and replaced with single dangling light bulbs; the walls were painted over in somber shades of gray, brown, and beige; and several of the lush trees in the garden were chopped down and the white marble swimming pool—whose ledges still protrude out from the now dusty playground—was filled with concrete to make ample space for a playground.

In stark contrast to the exquisitely crafted villa with its customized Italian marble floors and columns, curved oak staircase, sculpted moldings, and stain glass windows, stood a modern cement addition, a two-story rectangular building situated along the outer border of the courtyard facing the street. Its fourteen classrooms were uniformly painted with the bottom halves of the walls gray, and the top halves white. The villa, on the other hand, contained eight classrooms, the administrative offices, library, computer, media, environment, and home economics rooms.

Like so many schools in Egypt, this particular school operated in two shifts. Due to the population pressure on the public school system, a large percentage of school facilities serve as two and sometimes three separate schools. In Cairo, 54 percent of government primary schools (Grades 1–5), and 64 percent of government preparatory schools (Grades 6–8) are shift schools, figures that roughly correspond to the national average (Ministry of Education 1997, 15–16). The facility under study served as the Zahra School for Girls from 6:45 a.m. to 12:00 p.m. and as the Amira School for Girls from 1:00 p.m. to 6:00

p.m. (pseudonyms). In the interest of equity, the schools switched shifts in midyear; Amira School took the morning shift, and Zahra School the afternoon shift. Each shift was accompanied by a change in the name of the school and an entirely different school administration, staff, and students. The students' uniforms even differed from one shift to the other. The doorman (*bawaab*) and a single custodian were the only individuals common to both shifts.[7]

Approximately fifteen hundred students attended each school, or shift, making for a total of three thousand students who utilized the school facility each day. The class size was up to eighty pupils per class, far exceeding the national average of forty-one pupils per class (NCERD 1996, 40). Three, and sometimes four girls shared bench desks intended for two students.

Given the intensive use of the physical facility, a high degree of wear and tear was inevitable. However, certain aspects of the school facility jeopardized the overall physical and psychological well-being of the school community. On an average day twelve hundred students attended classes in the villa and ascended and descended the central winding staircase several times. The wooden steps were severely sunken, even crumbled in places. A dimly lit back stairway leading to attic classrooms and utilized by four hundred twenty girls on a daily basis, was in and alarming state of decay. The wooden steps were so frayed that in certain places one's foot could actually slip though them. This stairway, as one teacher put it, was "a catastrophe waiting to happen." The tiled floors in the classrooms and hallways were lopsided and warped from years of wear and resulted in a teacher tripping and breaking her leg. Classroom doors didn't close properly and outside noise disturbed the lessons. Broken windows let in cold air in the winter causing girls to catch colds. Classrooms tucked away in the basement or attic lacked fans and sufficient ventilation and the stuffy rooms were potential carriers of contagious illnesses. The lighting in much of the villa was insufficient; in several classrooms, a single dangling light bulb provided the room's only light and several corridors were unlit.

As for the classrooms, no one was certain when they were last painted, but their appearance indicated years, possibly even decades, of neglect. The severely pockmarked, smudged and gouged dark green and brownish walls were covered with hundreds of nails, staples, and tacks. In some rooms, students tacked brightly colored wrapping paper of pink teddy bears or birthday balloons around the walls in an effort to provide a more cheerful atmosphere.

The toilet facilities stood out as perhaps the worst example of neglect. Out of the eight toilets, five of them floor-level flush latrines, not one was functioning on the day the three-member neighborhood committee made our initial visit to the school. The plumbing system was blocked up, all the flushes were broken, and the floors were soiled with sewerage. These were the only toilet facilities available for the three thousand adolescent girls who attended the school each day, making for a ratio of one toilet per three hundred seventy-five students.

Senior administrators from both shifts, when asked about how the facilities had become so run-down, cited restraints having to do with finances and the low socioeconomic and cultural background of students. The school's maintenance budget allowed for only one full-time custodian and she was unable to cope with the onerous demands of cleaning the school grounds single-handedly. What's more, she received a salary of only LE 90 per month ($27), was in ill health, and at the time of our initial school visit, was eight months pregnant. The school administrators explained that the students were mainly from deprived social backgrounds, lived largely in urban poor areas that lacked modern amenities, and were not raised with values of caring for and respecting public property. The vice principal noted, for example, that they had given up repairing the toilets because the girls simply failed to clean up after themselves and didn't know how to properly use the flushes.

Some teachers, however, when pressed to explain the causes of facility neglect provided a different interpretation of the situation. Certain younger female teachers in particular argued that the students did not inherently suffer from sociocultural deficiencies, but could learn to care for their environment. They pointed out that certain basic features of the school facility and grounds needed to be improved and repaired to make it worthy of their care.

Having established that both the need and desire to improve the conditions of the school facility existed, the neighborhood volunteers (heretofore referred to as the neighborhood committee), set about making inquiries for raising funds and forming partnerships to begin a participatory intervention on the school environment. A member raised funds in the amount of $10,000 that could be used in any manner relating to school facility upgrade, however the initiative could not proceed without the authorization and support from key players within the educational establishment.[8]

Partnerships for Participation: Working within a Centralized Bureaucracy

> The [action researcher] must be committed to seeing the partici-
> patory research process through to the end, avoid actions that
> endanger community members, and see clearly, and support, the
> situation of the subordinate groups within the community....
> The researcher can make a significant contribution...by bring-
> ing new information, and helping to find funds for development
> or technical skills.
>
> —(Budd Hall 1981)

The action researcher working in schools within centralized systems of the type we find in Egypt, in addition to bringing a sense
of commitment, flexibility, goodwill, and access to resources and
information, must also possess a firm understanding of the power
and bureaucratic structure within which schools are located. In centralized systems with heavily bureaucratized management structures
it is essential, for the feasibility of a project and protection of all
participants involved, that any undertaking with a public sector
school involves the authorization and support of at least three key
people: a representative from the Ministry of Education; a representative from the local educational governorate (*mudariyya*); and the
headmaster/ mistress at the school. Persons from these three
domains, beginning with the relevant figure at the MOE, should be
informed in writing of the objectives of the initiative (however ten-
tative or process oriented it may be), the names of anyone outside
the school involved in the project, and its sources of funding. Three
individuals proved key in approving, legitimizing, supporting, and
directing various aspects of this initiative; the Undersecretary to the
Minister of Education who provided the official approval for the
project, a district supervisor for the Environment, and the headmaster of the afternoon shift.

The district supervisor for environment studies, Mrs. Alia, acted as
the Ministry's liaison to ensure the project remained within its stated
objectives. Due to her busy schedule and responsibility for fifty other
schools, she could not get involved in the day-to-day decision-making
or implementation of the project, but she served as a figurehead legitimizing it. Mr. Mustafa, the headmaster of Amira School, was a highly

committed educator in his late fifties. During the course of this initiative
he was suffering from poor health and was undergoing chemotherapy,
yet he made an appearance at work everyday and attended to all school
matters with diligence. We spoke with him at length about our understanding of participatory development and how we hoped to involve the
teachers and students in all stages of the initiative. He listened politely
and nodded his head in agreement, but would invariably present us with
lists, which he composed single handedly, of areas he identified for repair
along with price quotes for hiring professional workers. We tried to persuade him of the efficacy of students and teachers getting involved in the
process of both identifying problem areas in the school and in redressing
them. While he wasn't entirely convinced that participation was the most
efficient way of repairing the school, with time, many friendly discussions, and compromises on both sides, he opened the way for us to work
with school staff and students and gave teachers the green light to cooperate with us.

The headmistress of the other shift, Mrs. Nadia, was not enthusiastic
about the initiative. She maintained that it detracted students from academic studies and was a waste of time. Despite the efforts of the community volunteers and Mrs. Alia to try to persuade her to at least give it a
try, she remained unreceptive. Mrs. Alia, speaking on behalf of the
Ministry, explained to her that while she might not share the ideals of
the project, she was obliged to cooperate with it. Regrettably the neighborhood committee had little choice but to work with an unwilling part-
ner, and having to recognize that a project that involved forced
participation presented a serious dilemma—not one easy to resolve—to
the participatory approach.

Gender on the Job: Women and Men Relating to the Workplace

> I am obviously concerned about rendering our society more
> compassionate, more caring.... But it is hard to say that women
> would be better at changing things than men. If caring is linked
> to the maternal only, there are hard times ahead of us.... Many
> [men] have the same capacity. Much has to do with context,
> rearing, even class.
>
> —Maxine Greene, *Education, Power, and
> Personal Biography* (1998)

Having obtained the necessary permissions and made contact with Ministry personnel who would oversee the upgrading initiative, the neighborhood committee began working more intensively within the school community. The headmaster and district supervisor convened general meetings with the entire school staff to allow for collective discussions about possible directions the initiative could take. Initial brainstorming meetings with teachers and staff took place during the summer term when students were on holiday but teachers were required to make daily appearances at school. As work schedules are more fluid during the summer, it was relatively easy to coordinate joint meetings with teachers from both shifts, a feat that would prove increasingly difficult during the teaching terms.

The general meetings provided a forum for teachers to express their concerns about the school, get involved in finding viable ways of addressing them, and prioritizing how the project funds should be expended. From the first meeting a striking polarization emerged along gendered lines. In a classic public/private dichotomy, the male members of staff were overwhelmingly concerned with the public image and appearance of the school, while the women's preoccupation was more with its interior spaces and its effects on students and fellow colleagues.

The areas identified for repair by the male staff, from the junior teachers to the headmaster, included painting the outer walls of all buildings and repairing the street-side broken windows. The headmaster, defending what came to be the male position, reasoned: "Everyone sees the outside and it is better protected than the inside. Inside the girls touch and ruin everything. Anyway, very few people see the inside of the school." In contrast to the men, the women raised substantially different priorities. Rather than the public façade of the building, they expressed concern about the sanitation, safety, and physical and psychological health of the students and teachers. They identified the dangerous stairway, defective lavatories, broken windows, and the dimly lit, grim, and poorly ventilated classrooms as priorities for improvement. The student committees, when they were later brought into the decision making process, stressed the classrooms as their principle concern.

After several months of meetings and negotiations between the neighborhood committee, the district supervisor, school staff and students, a compromise plan of action was formulated: the project funds would be used to paint the outside wall, paint classrooms, replace the broken windows, restore the back stairway, rewire the electricity for improved lighting throughout the school, and repair classroom doors. Separate funds provided by the MOE maintenance section would be used to repair the toilet facilities, which were eventually fully refurbished. Having gotten over the hurdle of agreeing on a plan, the next challenge proved enlisting volunteers to carry it through.

Reluctant Participants

> Without infinite patience it is impossible to get the people to do any work...for [i]t is the reformer who is anxious for the reform, and not society, from which he should expect nothing better than opposition, abhorrence and even mortal persecution. Why may not society regard as retrogression what the reformer holds as dear to life itself?
> —Mohandas K. Gandhi, *An Autobiography:The Story of My Experiment with Truth* (1957)

Participatory development should ideally originate as an organic movement from within; within a village, a neighborhood, a factory, a school. Yet in reality there are often reformers who enter communities with fairly formed notions about what needs to be done and how to go about doing it. In this case the neighborhood committee consisted of three long-term residents of Cairo who lived in the neighborhood where the school was located and had previous experience in advocacy and development work. We had idyllic visions of students, teachers, and neighborhood residents working in harmony over several weekends painting classrooms, tiling floors, creating murals on the outside school walls, pulling weeds, and planting gardens. We anticipated that we would smoothly form partnerships with students and teachers who would share our enthusiasm. Needless to say, the process did not quite unfold as we had expected.

While teachers were forthcoming about attending brainstorming and planning meetings held during working hours, they were reluctant to commit to any activity that made additional demands on their time. Up to 80 percent of the teachers of core academic subjects worked extended hours after school giving private lessons, a highly common practice in Egypt. Still others took on disparate second jobs to supplement their paltry teacher's income which starts as low as $30 per month.

Women without outside jobs often had childcare and domestic responsibilities awaiting them after work. Overextended and underpaid, few teachers were prepared to commit their time to more than providing suggestions during in-school discussion sessions.

Faced with a dearth of teacher volunteerism the district supervisor and senior administrators enlisted the help of four vocational education teachers, all unmarried men in their early twenties and graduates of technical secondary schools who teach a course in maintenance. Maintenance has been a required subject for all middle schools since 1997 and deals with basic household maintenance. It meets for one forty-five minute period per week and includes lessons on topics such as electricity and simple carpentry. The teachers of maintenance are expected to have both theoretical and applied skills in building and grounds maintenance.

In conversations with the senior administrators, it also transpired that the maintenance teachers were selected for reasons having to do with class and gender. Occupying a lower social position than teachers of core academic subjects, the headmaster explained that the maintenance teachers were more in need of the bonus pay which would be offered them for their efforts in the initiative. For their participation in this project, they would receive a monthly bonus of LE 20. As men, they were considered more suitable than women or girls to carry out work involving painting and building repairs. Hence, the administrators were reinforcing the types of class and gender stereotypes that we, the neighborhood committee, were hoping to overcome. Despite being singled out for the work, the male vocational teachers wanted nothing to do with the project and actively refused involvement.

To understand the inactivity of the vocational education teachers necessitates a context of the standing, both historically and in contemporary Arab/Egyptian society, of vocational education. Vocational education suffers from low status in the overall hierarchy of formal schooling. As Al Hetti and Brock point out in their discussion of vocational education in the Arab states, there has been a long standing cultural bias in Arab societies against manual labor and, by extension, schooling that is directed toward labor oriented professions (1997, 373–374). The fact that low performing or substandard students get tracked out of general education and into less prestigious vocational or technical education schools reinforces its already low-ranking status (Al Hetti and Brock 1997, 379). Within the pecking order of a general middle school, the vocational teachers, holders of diplomas from technical secondary schools rather than universities, and teachers of technical, as opposed to the core academic subjects, occupy the lowest professional strata of teachers and receive the lowest salary.

The four vocational teachers eventually expressed in clear terms that they did not want to get involved in the initiative because they worried that appearing before their fellow colleagues and students as manual laborers would only serve to further reduce their status. One teacher, fearing that involvement in the initiative would mean he would have to personally paint the classrooms said, "I cannot hold a paint brush in my hand. I won't do that. It's not my job and I've gotten far from that." He added that he would be willing to supervise workers, tell them what to do, but he would not actually perform any of the labor himself.

Another teacher raised the issue of how he would lose his authority as a teacher if his students were to see him performing lowly manual work. "I teach these girls" he implored. I'm their teacher! I cannot let them see me doing the work of any painter. How will they regard me later when I'm standing before them in the classroom? They won't have respect for me and then I won't have any authority over them."

Without the involvement of the vocational teachers the initiative seemed at a temporary standstill. Pressured by the district supervisor and headmaster to deliver on some aspect of school improvement, the neighborhood committee reluctantly consented to hire an outside contractor to prepare and paint a single model classroom. It was hoped that a tangible change would generate more active participation from the school community.

The Colors of Change: Students and Teachers
Enter the Participatory Process

> Children...since they do not yet grasp our social practices as inevitable,...do not see why they might not do things differently."
>
> —Terry Eagleton, *The Significance of Theory* (1990)

In anticipation of the outside contractor, the NGO committee held several meetings with members of the school staff to discuss the issue of color. Each meeting proved brief as there was an overwhelming, undisputed consensus that the room should be painted gray. Occasionally there was some discussion as to the shade of gray that should be used, and whether the entire wall or only the lower half of the wall, and how much of the lower wall should be painted gray, however not a single staff

member so much as hinted that a color other than gray should be considered. Gray, we were told, absorbed glare and was the standard color of
Egyptian classrooms. While a perfectly rational explanation, it didn't
entirely explain the unanimous lack of any alternative opinions regarding
color. The acceptance of gray seemed in part indicative of how education
professionals internalize technocratic thinking that inhibits innovation or
change. Youth, on the other hand, are more likely to initiate new ways of
interacting with their environment since they do not yet see the older
ways as inevitable or immutable.

On a Friday morning, the only holiday in the school week,
Headmaster Mustafa arranged for an outside contractor to bring his crew
to the school to replaster and paint the walls of a single classroom. Two
students from the class and two members of the neighborhood committee, Sarah and I, were also present at the school that morning. We had
not yet settled the question of color, but were not surprised when
Mohammed the contractor spread his sampler of over one hundred
colors on Mr. Mustafa's desk and offered his professional opinion: "How
about this one?" he said pointing to a shade of light gray. Sarah and I
asked if we could get a second opinion and went to consult with the students who were waiting downstairs by their classroom. We showed two
eleven-year-old girls the color sampler and asked them what color they
would like for their classroom walls. They inspected the colors, con-
sulted each other in whispers and then, in a united gesture, both pointed
to the mauve. "This is nice, don't you think?" We commended their
choice. We asked Mr. Mustafa if he would approve their choice of color
and with a shrug of his shoulders and half-hearted smile, he consented.

On the following morning the new mauve classroom caused a stir.
The students were giddy with delight and a stream of teachers passed by
to inspect the room. The newly plastered and freshly painted mauve
walls dramatically brightened the interior space and contributed to an
almost immediate change of perception about the project. Teachers, who
previously were only vaguely interested in the upgrading initiative, came
forward with a desire to get more actively involved, as it had gone
beyond talking, meeting, and seeming endless planning, to a phase of
concrete results and possibilities. It became increasingly apparent that
color served as a catalyst for students and teachers to engage in a form of
praxis—of critically thinking and reflecting on the world in order to
change it. If one could change the technocratic gray color of the rooms,
then perhaps other aspects of schooling could be changed as well; the
notion was now in the realm of possibility. Through the simple act of

allowing the students a say in the color of their classroom, the participatory process was advanced considerably.

With the momentum high, a second classroom was immediately selected for painting. During a school day the work crew transferred their ladders and equipment from the ground floor to an upstairs classroom temporarily dislocating seventy-five students to the courtyard. The girls sat chatting on benches arranged in a u-shape. Seizing the opportunity of having them together, the contractor Mohammed, a maintenance teacher Tareq, and I explained to the students that their classroom was going to be painted and that they could select its color. On hearing this news they gasped excitedly, some jumped to their feet and began shouting out colors: "red," "lavender," "peach," "blue," "rose! " A throng of enthusiastic girls soon formed around Mohammed who held the color sampler and they tugged at his arm to get a closer look it. When they were calm and seated, the girls were given a choice of colors and voted on them. An enthusiastic Arabic teacher (and previous advocate of gray), offered her opinion that the peachy salmon color selected was "chic awi" or "very chic." That color won the day. While the process of color selection was not as orderly as it might have been, the girls were delighted to have input in the process.

Several female teachers became more forthcoming about suggesting various colors for the other rooms. Instead of gray, they requested mauve, salmon, and rose. "Did you see that classroom" a teacher asked referring to a mauve classroom, "it's so attractive, open, and light. Can we paint the activity room the same color?" Others asked where the contractor purchased the paint because they wanted to paint a certain room in their home the same color. Months later, when we were planning a second phase of the project which would include painting the library, Mme. Alia, one of the earlier proponents of gray classrooms, vehemently protested when the librarian requested to have the library painted white. "What? White?! Is this a hospital? Do you want the library to look like a bathroom?" Mme. Alia pulled her by the arm to the center of the salmon colored office and said, "Look how fresh and lovely this room looks. Don't you think this color would suit the library much more than white?" The librarian maintained that a bright white would be more suitable for the library.

With the growing interest generated over the choice of color, a core group of six young women teachers emerged as especially active and committed participants in the project. All in their early to mid-20s, they included teachers of core academic subjects (math and science), as well as teachers of noncore activities (*nashat*) such as media, environmental studies, home economics, and art. They were forthcoming about choosing colors for the hallways and activities' rooms, and organized what would be the Friday work camps (*maaskar 'amal*).

During a meeting leading up to the first work camp, I asked this group whether they were uneasy with the prospect of their students seeing them perform manual work such as painting or cleaning the school grounds. The question was especially intended for the teachers of the activities subjects whose academic credentials were similar to those of the male maintenance teachers. These women exhibited a markedly different attitude. The media teacher shook her head emphatically and answered "No, not at all. We do these things in our homes and this school, since it's a place we spend a lot of our time, is like our home. The girls understand that." I related how the male teachers were uneasy about their students seeing them hold paint brushes or engaging in other types manuel work and asked what they thought accounted for the difference in attitude between them. "They're men!" exclaimed the media teacher, "That's why they think like that. But don't worry" she continued menacingly shaking her index finder, "Leave it to us. We know how to get them to hold paint brushes in their hands!" The other teachers laughed and slapped each other's palms in playful communion.

Much has been made in feminist literature about how schooling, with its "hidden curriculum" serves to disadvantage women by reproducing sexual divisions of labor that assign women domestic and motherhood roles (Bennett and LeCompte 1990; Stromquist 1990). There has been an assumption, in other words, that the apparatus of formal education tends to perpetuate the public/private dichotomy in which men prepare for professional lives in the public domain, while women are relegated to roles in the private sphere. While this may often be the case, it can also transpire that when women ascribe domestic qualities to their work place, the professional community of both women and men can be considerably enriched.

Between (Dis)-Order and Discipline

> [In the third quarter of the19th century Egypt] streets and schools were built as the expression and achievement of an intellectual orderliness, a social tidiness, a physical cleanliness,

> that was coming to be considered the country's fundamental
> political requirement.... The space, the minds, and the bodies
> all materialised at the same moment, in a common economy of
> order and discipline.
> —Timothy Mitchell, *Colonising Egypt,* 1988

In his account of the genesis of modern, or new order, schooling in Egypt, Timothy Mitchell suggests that schools contributed to disciplining populations. Inspired by the work of Michel Foucault (1977), Mitchell posits that schools, by regimenting space and time through practices such as lining up desks and students in straight rows, and adhering to strict timetables, served to instill in youth a deep-rooted sense of orderliness (1988). Based on practices in many public sector schools today, schools have partially achieved goals of ordering and disciplining, but not entirely, for they can also be the sites, especially during nonacademic activities, of mass disorder and chaos.

Order and disorder were clearly displayed in the everyday life of Amira and Zahra schools. In the morning, students regularly lined up in orderly rows, paraded up to their classes in single file, arranged themselves in an organized fashion in severely overcrowded classrooms, and sat relatively quietly at their desks throughout the duration of their lessons. The moment the bell signaling the break rang, however, a general sense of chaos often broke out. Girls rushed towards narrow doorways often shrieking and not giving way to each other, and peeled down the stairway into the courtyard pushing one another and tripping along the way. In the corner of the courtyard next to the canteen, rather than line up for their turn to purchase a snack, the students crowded frantically around the food vendor in a semicircle, shoving each other combatively, waving money in outstretched hands toward the seller shouting, "Me next, Me next!" Yet with the sound of the yard monitor's whistle they tossed their empty potato chip and biscuit wrappers aside and ran to their assigned lines where they stood quietly before strutting, again in an orderly fashion, back to their classrooms. In an instant, with the blow of a whistle, clang of a bell, sound of a teacher's voice, the students' behavior was instantly transformed from disorder to order.

Given the potential for chaos, senior administrators expressed reservations about students being allowed too large a role in the work camps. Despite predictions by teachers that parents would not consent to their daughters joining the work camp because it involved performing manual work, and that was not the task of educated schoolgirls, there was overwhelming parental support. Not only did all the parents of the one hundred selected girls swiftly return their consent forms, but several parents called the school to inquire why their daughters had not been chosen.

The senior administrators were especially opposed to the idea of students painting their own classrooms. The vice headmistress explained that the girls would make a complete mess of the rooms and said they would "turn the world upside down!" Mr. Mustafa worried about safety hazards and would not consent to students climbing ladders and handling paint buckets. We reached a compromise and decided that the workers would carry out the major painting and repairs, including major carpentry and electrical work, and the students would paint the blackboards and varnish the desks, stairways, wood paneling and doors.

The work camps took place over three weekends with a deliberate decrease in participants each time. The first camp consisted of ten neighborhood volunteers, one hundred students, thirty teachers, and four parents who accompanied their daughters out of curiosity. Despite the critical importance of parents to the school community, the school committee decided to gain more experience with the mechanics of school upgrading before mobilizing parents. The majority of teachers in attendance were from Mr. Mustafa's shift, yet roughly two thirds of them arrived in formal clothing and spent the morning upstairs in the staff room drinking tea and chatting with their colleagues. Many teachers, it later surfaced, attended the work camp only because they were allowed to choose a day off anytime during the semester.

The most active members of the teacher committee were, predictably, the core group of female teachers mentioned above and, somewhat surprisingly, two of the maintenance teachers who had earlier withdrawn from the initiative. True to their promise, the female teachers persuaded their male colleagues to join them. With the energetic female teachers working beside them as a team, teasing and cajoling them, the men's attitudes and behavior changed dramatically. They enthusiastically partook in the varnishing of desks, painting, and collecting of trash and debris in and around the school grounds, joking and smiling sheepishly on hearing the bravos and encouragement from their female colleagues. The students, for their part, exhibited effusive enthusiasm and wholeheartedly, if somewhat noisily and at times chaotically, carried out work ranging from sweeping the building, varnishing desks and wood paneling, painting, collecting trash, and rearranging desks and furniture. While there may not have been ordered precision to the camp, there were definitely results and a strong show of commitment, particularly on the part of students: out of one hundred girls selected to take part in the first work camp, ninety-nine arrived to school on time.

Yet there were undeniably moments when students' enthusiasm proved difficult to manage. As the work camps were set on weekends in an informal setting, they lacked the familiar institutionalized methods of bringing students to order. Although the teachers and NGO committee held planning meetings to organize activities, the camps took on a momentum of their own. In the morning of the first camp, for example, Miss Azza, the environment teacher, tried to keep the girls in order while waiting for teachers to arrive, or in the case of those who already arrived, to finish drinking their tea. The students were getting restless so she selected ten of them to begin varnishing the main stairway. Those selected let out hoots of delight, while the others immediately began protesting "It's not fair Miss. Why can't we go?" Only minutes after the first set of ten girls began stroking the dry crumbling wooden paneling along the stairway with a shiny coat of varnish, a troupe of more girls rushed up the stairs excitedly screeching that they wanted a turn. Soon after another set of girls came running up the stairs causing a commotion. Girls began squabbling, knocking over cans of varnish, snatching brushes out of each other's hands, and shouting, "It's my turn, it's my turn"! Not able to control the situation that seemed to be turning dangerously out of order, I rushed to the teacher's room, clouded in cigarette smoke, pleading for help. Three of the older women teachers rushed to the stairs and slapped girls on their backs while shouting, "Get down, get out of here you animals!" Some girls retreated outside but moments later returned. We suspended all work until enough adults were available to take responsibility for groups of ten girls each.

Subsequent work camps were smaller and better organized. The tasks shifted from painting and building maintenance to cleaning the areas in and around the school facility. Students, teachers, and neighborhood volunteers met on Friday mornings to pick up and dispose of heaps of foil wrappers, plastic cups, broken bricks, cement tiles, scraps of wood and iron, and other trash that littered the outside wall and neighboring area. During each work camp the volunteer group ventured farther from the direct perimeters of the school to the nearby streets making for a sense of community responsibility. The processes leading up to and culminating in the community work camps, while representing an important milestone in the initiative, represented one stage in the overall process. In many respects the real challenges having to do with upkeep and sustainability were to come.

Follow-up and Sustainability

In the months following the work camps, the overall cleanliness of the school improved markedly. Headmaster Mustafa helped maintain the momentum by encouraging and praising the core teacher committee who regularly gathered students to pick up rubbish and keep their classrooms orderly and tidy. Likewise, students more actively looked after the building and grounds. A teacher observed that since the classrooms had been painted her students were much more willing, even vigilante, about taking care of them. Another teacher remarked that the girls were gaining a sense of pride in their school; on several occasions she overheard them stopping students from writing on the walls or tossing their trash on the floor.

Students themselves commented on how they enjoyed school much more. "The school is so much more comfortable," said one girl, "I actually like coming here now, unlike last year when I was absent a lot." Another student remarked, "I feel so relaxed at school this year, it feels brighter and more open." Such positive attitudes, accompanied by behavioral changes, were reinforced through structured activities organized by teachers and senior staff around the school environment.

Miss Mona, the media teacher, chose "the school environment" as a topic for the school magazine, a wall magazine of stories and news items written by students and posted on a school wall for anyone to read. This provided the opportunity for students to reflect on and articulate what it was they desired for their school and how they thought they could go about attaining it. Teachers also organized a school-wide competition for the most beautiful and cleanest classroom. The students scrubbed and decorated their classrooms by garnishing the doors with fresh flowers, hanging lace curtains over the windows, displaying their own artwork, making small medicine cabinets with emergency supplies, and stringing balloons and multi-colored foil across the walls. Some truly remarkable student artwork was displayed such as a list of students' names woven into a floral bouquet, and hand painted geography and astronomy posters. A delegation consisting of the vice principal, the social services officer, the head environment teacher, and myself took a tour of each classroom, voicing praise and encouragement to students for their efforts. Each room received an overall grade in cleanliness, artistry and safety and three prizes were awarded. The neighborhood committee held a ceremony and distributed small gifts to all the teachers who participated in the initiative. The school also gained public recognition for their efforts when the director from the local education district awarded a first prize certificate to the school for being the cleanest school in the district.

Despite the efforts of staff and students from Mr. Mustafa's shift (shift one), to beautify and maintain a clean environment at their school, they were unable to generate commitment in their counterparts on the other shift (shift two).

Staff and students from shift one expressed frustration with the obstructive attitude of shift two, but were determined to persevere and maintain a tidy and pleasant environment for themselves even if it meant grudgingly cleaning up the messes left behind by their second shift colleagues. Having experienced the benefits of school beautificaiton, they were determined to foster more cooperative relations with their shift two counterparts. They enlisted the help of the district supervisor Mrs. Alia, who headed a fifteen member in-school committee consisting of teachers and administrators from both shifts. The meetings were held between the two shifts, at the neutral hour of 12:00 to 1:00. The shift two headmistress consistently missed meetings because she was not willing to spend her time on these "extras." Her teachers were reticent to get too involved without her support. Despite their many efforts to involve the other shift, the staff from shift one, convinced of the many benefits of a beautified and clean environment, vowed to carry on with the initiative alone if necessary.

The shift one staff repeatedly expressed the hope that the MOE would fulfill its pledge to build more schools and eliminate the shift system altogether so that they could take full possession of their school. Nevertheless, in light of the decline in school buildings in recent years and the allocation of higher proportions of educational budgets to technology and equipment, the more basic needs in education—such as more school facilities—remain neglected. Clearly, many issues need to be addressed in the long term, such as how all students, teachers, administrators, and community members can resolve differences and take ownership and responsibility for their school; a public institution, a community fixture, a place of unbounded influence in the lives of so many people, not least the girls who spend a significant portion of their childhood and adolescence within its walls, among its neighborhood, in its community.

Conclusion: Building Community

> ... [A] sense of responsibility for the planet is born from a sense of responsibility for one's own neighborhood. It is hard to imagine that anyone who fouls his or her own nest could care very much about the tree in which it is lodged.... [W]e must... [invent] ways to engage students in the care of their own schools, neighborhoods, and towns.
> —Neil Postman, *The End of Education: Redefining the Value of School* (1995)

Whatever notions and visions for participatory development the NGO committee harbored before entering the school, through a process that included endless discussions, gaining familiarity with the lives of teachers and other school workers, disagreements, camaraderie, and conflict, they were substantially altered as the months passed. Two years into this initiative we can point to some tangible physical improvements in the school: the school building is far more attractive with its newly painted mauve and salmon colored classrooms and common areas; it is safer because the back stairway has been replaced, and better lighting has been installed throughout the corridors and classrooms.

Many students and teachers have repeatedly commented that the changes in the physical school facility, which they played an active role in achieving, have significantly improved their attitude toward their school and made them feel proud to be associated with it. Consequently they have made greater efforts to keep the school tidy and attractive and have been recognized for their efforts by being awarded a prize by the district office as the cleanest school.

Just as significant as the concrete physical gains, have been the subtle and immeasurable ones. The months of planning where nothing much appeared to be happening, in fact, yielded new ways of interpreting and acting on the social world of the school. The students in part spurred this process by bypassing gray and choosing other brighter and appealing colors for their classrooms. Color, in other words, served as a symbolic marker of change, a catalyst for students and teachers to go beyond technocratic approaches to schooling and engage in a form of praxis—or reflecting on their social world in order to change it. In other words, the notion of change entered the realm of possibility.

Similarly, the female teachers provided their male colleagues with new ways of relating to and thinking about their work environment. When women ascribed domestic qualities to their work place, the professional community as a whole was enriched. Remarkably, just months after declaring that they could not be seen publicly engaging in manual labor, two of the male vocational education teachers proudly engaged in clean-up activities in full view of their colleagues and students. As actions associated with the upgrading initiative took on a positive connotation, some teachers came to alter the ways in which they interpreted and acted on their world, demonstrating that socially constructed attitudes and roles associated with gender, age, and professional status are not immutable.

The shortcoming of the initiative has clearly been that it has not been able to foster closer relations between the communities of the two shifts. As the members of shift one took a more concerted role in promoting ideals of self-reliance through maintaining, cleaning, and beautifying the school environment, they increasingly clashed with their second shift counterparts, some of whom considered school improvement a waste of time. In an ideal world, each school community would have its own school, however as long as resources do not allow for this, community based upgrading initiatives offers a partial and possible solution.

On a personal note, my relationship with the neighborhood changed profoundly after getting involved in this initiative. When out in the neighborhood, I frequently encounter students or teachers from the school and we share a smile or a chat. I pass the school with an ear to the familiar voices within it, and an eye to the care of the grounds. After years of living in the neighborhood, I have become a member of its community.

Notes to Chapter 6

1. This chapter is dedicated to the memory of Mr. Mustafa Baza, an exemplary Egyptian educator.

2. The members of the neighborhood committee, apart from the author, were Barbara Ibrahim and Sarah Buhari. The author would like to express warm thanks to them for earlier comments on this paper.

3. See (*Al Ahram Weekly* 1999; Middle East Times 1999).

4. Two recent national surveys dealing with adolescence and the school environment in Egypt document how the condition of a school facility contributes significantly to the overall experience of schooling and affects the psychological and physical well being of students and educators (El Tawila et al. 1999; El Tawila et al. 2000).

5. The community school movement, spearheaded by UNICEF in 1992 and which continues with vigor today, serves as a powerful example of how partnerships between international organizations, local NGOs, members of local communities, and the Ministry of Education can provide the force for sustained education and social reform (Zaalouk 2004).

6. Note that the United Nations International Women's Conferences have provided perhaps the most comprehensive policy recommendations—or Forward-Looking Strategies (FLS) for aiding states in developing policies to ensure more gender equitable approaches to education. Among the strategies most relevant for our purposes—a facility upgrade initiative at a girls' school— are those that relate to vocational education and the role of NGOs in development. In both the Nairobi 1985 and Beijing 1995 international meetings, the FLS recommended that women be provided with vocational training and construction and management skills, and that NGOs play a role in training women in "self-reliance and leadership" (Stromquist 1997, 206–207).

7. See Mark Bray's *Double-Shift Schooling: Design and Operation for Cost-Effectiveness* for a more comprehensive treatment of double-shift schooling worldwide (2000).

8. The regional director the West Asia and North Africa office of the Population Council at that time, Barbara Ibrahim, approached a senior ranking executive at the Egypt office of the international corporation General Electric requesting financial support for a pilot upgrading initiative at an Egyptian school and received a grant in the sum of $10,000.

References

Al Ahram Weekly. 1999. The Price of Neglect? 28 Oct.–3 Nov.

Al Heeti, Abdul G., and Colin Brock. 1997. Vocational education and development: Key issues, with special reference to the Arab world. *International Journal of Educational Development* 17(4): 272–389.

Bennett, Kathleen P., and Margaret D. LeCompte. 1990. *How schools work: A sociological analysis of education.* White Plains, NY: Longman.

Bray, Mark. 2000. *Double-shift schooling: Design and operation for cost-effectiveness.* 2nd edition. Paris: UNESCO/International Institute for Educational Planning.

Eagleton, Terry. 1990. *The significance of theory.* Cambridge, MA: Blackwell.

El Tawila et al. 1999. *Transitions to adulthood: A national survey of Egyptian adolescents.* New York: Population Council.

———. 2000. *The school environment in Egypt: A situational analysis of public preparatory schools.* New York: Population Council.

Foucault, Michel. 1977. *Discipline and punish: The birth of the prison.* Trans. Alan Sheridan. New York: Pantheon.

Freire, Paulo. 1970. *The pedagogy of the oppressed.* Trans. Myra Bergman Ramos. New York: Seabury.

Gadotti, Moacir. 1994. *Reading Paulo Freire: His life and work.* Trans. John Milton. Albany: State University of New York Press.

Gandhi, Mohandas. K. 1957. *An Autobiography: The story of my experiment with truth.* Boston: Beacon Hill.

Greene, Maxine. 1998. "Interview." In 159–182. *Education power, and personal biography*, ed. Carlos A. Torres. New York and London: Routledge.

Hall, Budd. L. 1981. Participatory research, popular knowledge and power: A personal reflection. *Convergence* 14(3): 6–18.

Middle East Times. 1999. School wall collapse shakes Zamalek. 29 October.

Ministry of Education. 1997. *Pre-university education.* Cairo: Ministry of Education.

Mitchell, Timothy. 1988. *Colonising Egypt.* Cambridge: Cambridge University Press.

National Center for Educational Research and Development (NCERD). 1996. *Development of education in Arab Republic of Egypt: 1994/95–1995/96.* Cairo: NCERD.

————. 2001. *National report of Arab Republic of Egypt from 1990 to 2000.* Cairo: NCERD.

Postman, Neil. 1995. *The end of education: Redefining the value of school.* New York: Alfred A. Knopf.

Stromquist, Nelly, P. 1990. Gender inequality in education: accounting for women's subordination. *British Journal of Sociology of Education.* 11, no. 2, 137–153.

————. 1997. Gender sensitive educational strategies and their implementation. *International Journal of Education Development* 17, no. 2, 205–214.

Zaalouk, Malak. 2004. *The pedagogy of empowerment: Community schools as a social movement in Egypt.* Cairo and New York: American University in Cairo Press.

Conclusion: The Struggle for Democratic Education in the Arab World

CARLOS ALBERTO TORRES

The Great Questions

> I am not impartial or objective; not a fixed observer of facts and happenings. I never was able to be an adherent of the traits that falsely claim impartiality or objectivity. That did not prevent me, however, from holding always a rigorously ethical position. Whoever really observes, does so from a given point of view. And this does not necessarily mean that the observer position is erroneous. It's an error when one becomes dogmatic about one's point of view and ignores the fact that, even one is certain about his or her point of view, it does not mean that one's position is always ethically grounded.
>
> —(Freire 1998, 22).

Freire's epistemological and ethical dictum is useful here. We did not approach this research as indifferent observers who inspected Egyptian educational experiences: quite the contrary. Working from within the perspective of critical theory, we are committed to social transformation from an analytical and normative perspective, and therefore, we ground our ethical position in the need to ameliorate social injustice, to advance social and educational equity, and to promote—and learn through—dialogue and peace as a means of border crossing in education. A constant crossing of the lines of difference—whether racial, ethnic, gender, religious, social class or other—in the struggle for rationality, solidarity, and conviviality—or the tools of conviviality, if one may use Ivan Illitch's appropriate terminology—, is essential in our intellectual project.

Hence, the question of education is a question of democratic education. We wonder how the contributions of critical theory and critical pedagogy can help. Democratic education cannot be understood, in Egypt or elsewhere, without reference to human rights, an issue that in the context of authoritarian societies (or despotic societies, in the terminology of some authors), needs to be carefully analyzed. Coming back to a most important insight from Freire, can we practice a pedagogy of the oppressed in a context lacking basic democratic protections? Could we imagine experiences leading to cultural action for freedom, given the present situation of Arab societies engulfed, particularly after the invasion of Iraq, in a whirlwind historical process, which, in hindsight, may prove highly destabilizing for its structures, practices, and social movements?

Finally, in light of the lessons learnt in this study, one could and should ask how we can contribute to the betterment of educational experiences in Egypt and in the Arab world. This question needs to be addressed considering the politics of culture that prevail, the model of the state in which educational policies take place, and the actual outcomes of the educational experiences of pupils, teachers, administrators, and parents.

Overcoming Authoritarian Practices

> All pedagogical action is, objectively, symbolic violence insofar as it is the imposition of a cultural arbitrary by an arbitrary power"
>
> —(Bourdieu and Passeron 1990, 5).

One of my most vivid impressions as a Latin Americanist learning about the Arab world, is that the "Orientalist" tradition some scholars in the United States have delighted so much in promoting, conceives the Arab and Islamic region as so culturally unique that it cannot be comparable to the rest of the world. This is simply not so. The situation in the Arab world, in terms of its struggles against oppression, confrontations with a market mentality, and rising ideological religiosity, to name just a few factors, reflect changes in the larger world, and in many instances share a comparable focus and orientation.

While this book provides a window to life in Egyptian schools, there is a specific focus in several chapters on violence, punitive practices, and punishments. There is a critique of discipline in the classroom, and the difficulties teachers and administrators have in handling not only discipline in the classroom, but the secular principles imbued in the organization of educational systems. Egypt is, above all, a pious society, one that hinges on the importance of religion to articulate the different layers of social relationships. If there is a growing resentment towards authoritarian governments, while it may be on the surface expressed in religions terms, it is often a political response, and a social strategy for survival of the oppressed. I concur with Gita Sahgal and Nira Yuval-Davis when they define fundamentalism as "not referring to religious observance, which we see as a matter of individual choice, but rather to modern political movements which use religion as a basis for their attempt to win or consolidate power and extend social control" (2003, 43). They further argue:

> The rise of fundamentalism is linked to the crisis of modernity of social orders based on the belief in the principles of enlightenment, rationalism and progress. Both capitalism and communism have proved unable to fulfill people's material, emotional and spiritual needs. A general sense of despair and disorientation has opened people to religion as a source of solace. Religion provides a compass and an anchor; it gives people a sense of stability and meaning as well as a coherent identity. (Ibid., 45)

I have discussed the question of religion in another work (Torres 1992), and without repeating the arguments, it makes sense to underline two important elements of the connections between religion and education. The first is the question of a sense of direction in the people. With the great transitions in the latter part of the twentieth century (it will be sufficient to compare two world maps both before and after 1989 to see an impressionistic view of the transitions), and the growing work and existential insecurity of people in advanced industrial societies, and, as its darker counterpart, with the growing misery of millions in the Third World, it should come as no surprise that religion is playing such a politicized role. Thus, to continuously seek a definition of religious fundamentalism as an expression of barbarism or uncalled for radicalism is simply not to realize how the human condition has been threatened by changes in the political, economic, and cultural domains.

These changes have been brought about by the social transitions that came with the demise of socialism at a global scale, the increasing role of multinational /international organizations regulating capitalist exchanges that have eroded the power of the nation states, and the increased technological changes in the context of globalization. Thus, to put it simply, expect more religious fundamentalism as a response to the need to have, as Sahgal and Yuval-Davis say, a compass and an anchor in the changing and turbulent waters of today's unequal societies.

Yet, one could easily conclude that the rising costs of fundamentalist transitions and traditions, is to put at risk the same promise of democracy (fully embodied in the notion of public education), but above all, in the same promise of the Enlightenment (with the notion of modernity, rationalization, and progress, attributes and properties that were expected to be the product of modern education). Yet there is another important angle in this story, and it is the loss of meaning of schooling for children and youth in most places on Earth. One could resort to all sorts of anecdotes to substantiate this point, particularly the disarticulation of schooling with the growing and yet fragmented globalization of youth culture.[1] Let me, however, get back to the discussion of the connections between authoritarianism and education.

I grew up in an authoritarian society, Argentina. Reading the stories and listening to the voices presented in this book brought back memories. At the age of seven (second grade), I experienced a typical punishment to which some teachers submitted their students. A vignette will help to illustrate the point. Maestro M, a young, eighteen-year-old and fresh graduate from a normal secondary school, and with little training, was employed to teach second grade in a parochial Catholic school. In charge of forty-five students, Maestro M. resorted to violence, physical punishment, and torturous tools to control his students. He was a very tall, imposing young man. He would hit his students with his wooden pointer, or throw chalk or erasers at those who spoke out of turn, were distracted, or fell asleep in class. Occasionally, he would take the whole class to the patio of the school, have them line up facing the wall, and in typical military fashion, submit them to a sort of firing squad, with him kicking a soccer ball over their heads. The sound and closeness of the ball blasting the wall just above our heads, terrified us. He discontinued the practice when during the said torment, a student lost control of his bowels and had to call his mother to pick him up.

One day, maestro M. hit me on the head with an eraser when I was talking to one of my classmates. When the time came for the students to have their lunch, I joined the line of students who leave the school to lunch at home even though my mother, who had a small workshop at home, placed me with the group that lunches at school and remains there until late afternoon. Not wanting to go home against my mother's wishes, I loitered in the street during the lunch break. One of my neighbors found me and told me to return to school. I explained that my teacher hit me and that I didn't want to go back, so she took me home. I told my mother what happened and was surprised to see how much it upset her. After feeding me, my mother walked with me back to school. We went immediately to the Director's office, where she complained about the punishment. The Director, a religious Brother, was outraged, and summoned maestro M. to face my very upset mother. The Director told him, in very clear, stern terms, that his behavior was unacceptable and that if he ever hit another student he would lose his job. My mother, showing her own style of conflict resolution, told the Director and maestro M. that she decided to directly handle the problem herself rather than tell my father because he would never accept one of his children being physically punished and would express his rage violently. I remember experiencing a certain degree of satisfaction as I witnessed the dialogue, which I saw as a form of getting even with my teacher who abused me. Once my mother left and the Director returned to his other duties, maestro M. took me back to my class. Before we entered the classroom he stopped, looked down at me from what for me seemed an immense height, and asked, "Torres, why did you do this? You could have told me. We could have talked." I don't remember what I said, but I do remember that I had a most gratifying feeling, beating him and his oppressive tactics.

Fifteen years later, the story took a most interesting and eventful turn. It was 1971 or 1972, years of political crisis in Argentina, with the beginnings of guerrilla warfare, political agitation, and social mobilization against a military dictatorship that had ruled the country since 1966. The students had taken over and occupied the private Jesuit university where I studied and was one of the student leaders representing the School of Sociology. We wanted to revolutionize the university by linking it with the popular sectors, by changing the approach to science, and a host of other things. While the building was under our control, professors were not allowed to teach, and administrators were not allowed to enter until we could resolve our grievances. In fact, it was such a lengthy conflict that we created informal courses and enlisted sympathetic professors to teach them free of charge, with the intention of later trying to include these courses as part of the accepted curriculum. One evening, towards the end of one of the many meetings of student leaders in the central campus, a tall man approached me and asked, "Are you Torres? I was your teacher in second grade, remember me?" At that time maestro M. was the student leader of another faculty within the same university. We found ourselves in the same trenches and part of the same social movement. We hugged, had a brief conversation, and, in the end, he thanked me for what I did when I was seven years old. He told me, "you taught me a lesson."

Physical punishment in schools is an important issue, and the moral of this vignette is that children can defend themselves against abuse if they find a way to communicate their grievances to sympathetic adults. They can also play a role in guiding teachers' understandings of what constitutes acceptable discipline, of making them empathetic to their position. Experienced teachers will invariably resort to more sophisticated methods of discipline rather than physical punishment.

One of the key findings of this book, beyond corruption, violence, and authoritarianism in society and school classrooms, is that in Egypt, like most of the world, education is supposed to breed democracy and citizenship. The next section addresses the notion of critical theory as a way to deal with some of the dilemmas of a democratic education in nondemocratic societies.

Critical Pedagogy, Democracy, and Education

> Yo encaro esta relación dialéctica "vanguardia-masa" exactamente como Marx encaró la relación dialéctica "Pensamiento-ser subjetividad-objetividad teoría- práctica.
>
> (I face the dialectical relationship between "vanguard-people" exactly how Marx faced the pedagogical relationship "thinking-being, subjectivity-objetivity, theory-practice). (Translated by the author)
>
> —(Freire cited in Torres, 1978, 61)

What is the meaning and nature the concept of *critical* in critical social theory? Canadian critical theorist Raymond Morrow offers an insightful set of distinctions when he argues that:

> The term *critical* itself, in the context of 'Critical Social Theory' has a range of meanings not apparent in common sense where critique implies negative evaluations. This is, to be sure, one sense of critique in Critical Social Theory, given its concern with unveiling ideological mystifications in social relations; but another even more fundamental connotation is methodological, given a concern with critique as involving establishing the presuppositions of approaches to the nature of reality, knowledge, and explanation; yet another dimension of critique is associated with the self-reflexivity of the investigator and the linguistic basis of representation. (Morrow and Brown 1994, 7)

Knowledge construction, as Paulo Freire and others have taught us, should combine "the theoretical rigor of the social sciences in critic[al] dialogue with the living experience of the people" (Torres 1994, 20). Following Morrow's contribution, we would like to argue that as a research program, critical social theory implies several dimensions. It is a *human science*, hence providing a humanistic, antipositivist approach to social theory. It is a *historical science of society*, hence it is a form of historical sociology. Finally it is a *sociocultural critique* that is concerned with normative theory, that is, a "theory about values and what ought to be. Critical imagination is required to avoid identifying where we live here and now as somehow cast in stone by natural laws" (Morrow and Brown 1994, 11).

Yet there is no unitary critical social theory as Douglas Kellner forcefully argues in his comprehensive study of the critical tradition initiated by the Frankfurt School (1989). Another important insight from Kellner's analysis is the notion that critical social theory attempts a synthesis which, as a research program, can only be accomplished through collective groups of intellectuals aiming at social transformation:

> [A critical social theory] project requires a collective, supradisciplinary synthesis of philosophy, the science and politics, in which critical social theory is produced by groups of theorists and scientists from various disciplines working together to produce a Critical Social Theory of the present age aimed at radical social-political transformation. (Kellner 1989,7)

For the critical social theory tradition, theory cannot be easily separated from practice. Hence, a political sociology of education should improve not only the understanding of social reality (i.e., the project of the Enlightenment to enrich the knowledge of individuals and societies), or improve the epistemological, logical, and analytical perspectives of metatheory, theory, and empirical research (i.e., theorizing), but should also contribute to improving the practice of policy makers, policy brokers, and policy constituencies, and the cognitive and noncognitive outcomes of the process of teaching and learning. A byproduct of this discussion is the role of intellectuals employing critical social theory as opposed to liberal, neoliberal, and neoconservative intellectuals employing mainstream theories (Torres 1999).

Even having established the importance of critical theory for academic work, one could legitimately ask the question of what difference does our work as educators and researchers make? We struggle for achieving classroom environments embedded in democratic dialogues, classrooms where inequality doesn't take place, classrooms where racism, sexism, classism, sexual or religious discrimination—to name just a few of the educational problems—do not exist. We strive for educational environments where domination and exploitation are challenged by the logic of communicative rationality á la Habermas, hoping this practice will reach beyond the classroom into civil society and the state. For instance, in the United States many members of minority groups, and now, in growing numbers, female students join the Armed Forces where they endorse an ethic of destruction—honoring death as a way of life and accepting the glamour of war. Imagine (if this is the case in a society that prides itself on its democratic behavior), what the implications of these processes would be in authoritarian societies?

Make no mistake: critical educators ask challenging questions about education and democracy in the United States out of patriotism and transparency at a time when the Bush administration is pursuing policies of global hegemony and neoimperialism. Despite the growing conservative reaction to forms of criticism under the Bush regime, and despite efforts to instill fear in academia through policing and controls not seen since Macarthyism, criticism cannot be eliminated.[2] In times like these, more than ever, educators should take the lead from Paulo Freire, for whom their work and against whom their work is grounded. Freire's dictum is very much present in the analyses put forward by the educators and researchers contained in this book of the life in Egyptian schools.

Critical social theory offers important analytical tools and normative principles for a rigorous discussion about school governance and politics in the Arab world and provides a framework from which to understand and address issues of democratization, citizenship, and education. Yet by democratization, we are not referring to the type of electoral democracy imposed by military force. Indeed, things need to be placed in perspective. Given the neoimperialist position of the United States in the world system, an analysis grounded in critical social theory (CST) argues it is insufficient to claim that quality and equality of education should be achieved in the United States or elsewhere by eliminating discrimination and inequality based on class, gender, race, sexual orientation, or religion. Even if these processes of discrimination in formal education would, by some miraculous factor, disappear tomorrow or be drastically ameliorated, the more significant questions about democracy (or to be more precise, the lack of democratic behavior of the United States as the only remaining superpower), will continue to plague the work of conscious scholars who believe that social justice can only be achieved with peace. The notion of peace should be understood not as an instrumental reasoning or as a hegemonic model for settling disputes in the Middle East, but as a natural outgrowth of social arrangements that promotes equality of opportunity, equity in the social distribution of goods and services, and access to jobs, quality education, and healthcare, as well as social and political representation in the context of a radical democracy. Many of us think the role of education could make a difference.

Education, Democracy, and Citizenship

> You left us your scruples, testimony of an old fighter without concessions to capitalism, to injustice, to absent democracy, to oppression, to lovelessness, and the last of the demons you sought to exorcise, neo-liberalism
> —A verse from "Requiem por Paulo Reglus Neves Freire" (Torres 2004, 23)

From the perspective of critical theory, the relationship between education and democracy is problematic. It is already common sense in the sociology of education to argue that in order to achieve democratic education and citizenship the role of the state as a modernizer is paramount. Citizenship has always been associated with the constitution and operation of the modern nation state. Yet, the question remains of whether or not the nation state and citizenship are withering as the process of globalization accelerates. Egypt seems to prove Immanuel Wallerstein's argument that the history of the (capitalist) world system has been a historical trend towards cultural heterogeneity rather than cultural homogenization. Thus, the fragmentation of the nation in the world system is happening at the same time that there is a tendency towards cultural differentiation or cultural complexity (i.e., globalization). Globalization and regionalization seem to be dual processes occurring simultaneously (Wallerstein 2004).

In the past, the relationship between education and citizenship was understood as a very simple theoretical question. From an economic perspective, the question was how schooling should make labor highly skilled, and therefore more competitive. Facing the changes in the world system, the model was slightly modified to observe that if people are educated to think more analytically, rather than through a pedagogy that drills on skills, and that at the same time, people learn how to work on problem solving more collaborative (team work), then education will fulfill its economic role. It is exactly this reasoning, which is behind an agenda for educational change "that includes developing national standards for curriculum, student achievement, and teacher certification, and Europeanizing the school-to-career transition" (Weiner 1998, 185).

The question of linking this educational reform with the workings of democracy was simply stated as promoting a model of citizenship that will allow the educational system to meet the challenges posed to them by a democratic system based on citizenship demands and the demands of institutional capitalism. What was subtly understood in that model was that there is a perpetual tension between capitalism and democracy, which in turn affects the role of education (Torres 1998). However, that tension will go through a constant process of accommodation (Bowles and Gintis 1986), and a new resolution of this tension will emerge—in itself subject to further changes in the future given the notion of unstable equilibrium.

In neoliberal times, the main questions have to do with how globalization is affecting organized solidarity; how citizenship is being checked by market forces and globalization dynamics; and how democracy could be effective despite its ungovernability. It should not surprise the reader to learn that many of the dilemmas in this book as presented by teachers, administrators, and parents, fall squarely in these dilemmas of democracy and globalization. The unstable link between democracy and capitalism has been blurred to levels rarely seen before. Since capitalism has no alternative system to compete for recognition in terms of social organization of production and distribution worldwide, the democratic requirements for the operation of the capitalist system are being seriously criticized, particularly by neoconservatives that find democracy expensive and ungovernable. One may argue, however, that "When social movements press schools to live up to their democratic purposes, the struggles alter the relationship of social forces, exciting forces that can weaken capitalism's social and political hegemony." (Wiener 1998, 194).

In light of the evidence and the empirical practice of schooling in Egypt, one may consider the possibility that the bureaucratic interplay of the school system, even in highly regimented and authoritarian systems, has taken on a life on its own, yet, is not detached from the realm of hegemony (e.g., aspirations, expectations, intellectual orientation, or even the notion of common sense underlying the hegemony) of civil society. Lessons learned in this book show that parents want an education grounded in an Arab and Islamic identity. However, this still does not provide an answer to the key problematiques of the connection of democracy, education, and citizenship in an impoverished authoritarian society. This question cannot be addressed unless one takes seriously the problematique of human rights.

Human Rights and Education

As evidenced through the different chapters of this book, education in Egypt is a highly contested terrain. In a way, the overall process seems to be more personal than impersonal, or agency-oriented rather than structure-oriented, with the connection between teacher and student as paramount to pedagogical practice (for instance, the whole discussion about corporal punishment, or how teachers regard the presence of the Ministry of Education inspectors in the schools as an intrusion.)

Another important question is that cosmopolitanism, even in a society like Egypt, continues to play a major role in the ability of communities to succeed: rural communities continue to lag behind urban enclaves. The same could be said about class distinctions, which are reflected in the structural and segmented nature of the school system, with a growing private education model attending to the needs of the ruling elites and relegating public schooling as inhabited by the poor and the lower-middle classes. One should be careful, however, not to equate the growth of private education with the presence of a more sophisticated, demanding, and cosmopolitan middle class creating differential educational futures for differential occupational futures to their offspring. In Egypt, the growth of private education is located in a multitude of poor neighborhoods, and is sometimes connected with conservative Islamist politics, an educational orientation hardly regulated under the umbrella of state policies.

In short, in the context of disputes for identity, and the politics of culture as performed in social formations where racism and ethnic tensions, sexism and patriarchy, and class exploitation and patrimonialism persist, these factors cannot be ignored as part of the complex social, cognitive, and symbolic fabric constitutive of the daily experience of people, both at the level of the elites and within the socially subordinated sectors. In many of these respects, Egypt also reflects the current trends of the disputes for identity and the politics of culture that exist elsewhere. There should be no question that the overall expansion of schooling in Egypt, and the operation of such complex systems, is to some extent dependent on the legitimacy needs of the Egyptian state, and also the role that Egypt occupies in the Middle East and as an ally of the United States.

Many critics of Arab authoritarian states should remember that in the name of preserving universal human rights in the face of deteriorating societal and state conditions, atrocities have been committed by western societies supposedly creating the conditions to the inception of democracy. The United States is indeed a central international player in human rights abuses through its tactic of exporting democracy by waging war. 2005 marks the sixtieth anniversary of when the United States unleashed on civilians, not soldiers, the power of the atomic bomb in Hiroshima and Nagasaki, even though many analysts considered it unnecessary as the Japanese Empire was crumbling and about to lose the war. The violence of the atomic bomb killed and maimed scores of innocent civilians and generated conditions for the potential extinction of the human race. A similar level of violence and disrespect for human rights, in present-day Iraq, marks deeply the contradictions of democracy today.

The daunting images of the Abu Ghraib Prison human rights abuses, the condemnation by the Red Cross mission of the United States military detention center in Guantanamo with practices that are considered borderline with systematic torture (Amnesty International

2004), or the more evident fact that since the invasion of coalition forces led by the United States to Iraq, more than one hundred thousand Iraqis have been killed, either as a direct result of armed intervention, or as bystanders caught in the cross fire, should make us very worried about the practical possibility of succeeding in exporting democracy through violent means. While one should recognize that democracy cannot be exported through the carpet bombing of communities, by the same token, one should recognize that the experience of schooling, even in a fairly moderate state such as Egypt (a key ally of the United States in the Middle East), reflects a more complex picture than simply state-modernization of rational choice by individuals trying to maximize their options.

Even with their limited resources and the lack of imagination of a bureaucracy whose primary function seems to reproduce itself, schools continue to be a place for socialization, citizenship, and intellectual inquiry. If schools and universities are heavily regulated and regimented, these processes seem to be compatible to the basic structures of Egyptian society finding ways to accommodate the growing heterogeneity of society.

Where do we go from here?

> ... there is no document of civilization which is not at the same time a document of barbarism
> —(Benjamin 1968, 258)

In drawing conclusions from our studies, the first conclusion that needs to be highlighted is that education in the Arab world, if left to its self-contained dynamics, may not fulfill its democratizing potential. There are too many structural pressures, and above all, lack of financial and material conditions, for educational systems to achieve a level of maturity compatible with a notion of humanistic education (Gadotti 2004). We have to challenge the way in which we understand education because of its economic value. As I have argued elsewhere, "There is no reason to base all policy on economic rationality ignoring centuries of humanistic education, pedagogical research, or alternative models and critical perspectives" (Torres 2004).

One could speak of new conditionalities in external aid that could replace the rigid neoliberal conditionalities built into the loans of the

World Bank (Samoff and Caroll 2003; Torres 2004), or the external assistance to Egypt by the United States. Simple, small steps could be of great help. For instance, increasing the amount of resources devoted to empirical research in the schools, opening up school environments to critical scrutiny by parents, social movements, and NGO's, rather than data being totally controlled by bureaucracy. We should remember that while planning is an exercise of optimism, by and large data is a political prisoner of the governments.

In another place, the author has outlined some of the possible conditions to enhance the educational experience of democratic educational models leading to the promotion of citizenship. Seeking to promote civic virtues and multicultural democratic citizenship, I have argued that citizenship should be understood as civic virtues in the context of distributional policies and not merely as the conferring of status (Torres 1998). The argument here is that multicultural citizenship should not be considered a supplement to ordinary citizenship, but no real citizenship can be achieved unless contemporary capitalist societies and liberal democracies solve the problem of citizenship. It is because of the pitfalls of liberal democracy that we need to advocate a democracy with objectives, a radical democracy.

Among the key virtues of a radical democratic multicultural citizenship is the great learning of liberalism: tolerance. As Freire poses:

> I fulfill my mission as an educator when, 'fighting' to convince learners of the revelation of truth, I myself become transparent, allowing my students the possibility of arguing with the ideas of my discourse. I fulfill my mission as an education when I reveal, finally, my tolerance in the face of those who are different from me. (Freire 1998b, 4,)

Yet, a model of tolerance based on knowledge, discipline, and self-reflection is not sufficient for the exercise of democratic multicultural citizenship. We need, following one of the most important insights of Paulo Freire, an epistemology of curiosity, one that breaks loose the imagination of children and youths, that unwraps the inquisitive minds of teachers, so often subjugated by bureaucratic structures, rules and regulations, and that links science to the experience of the conscience of people. Perhaps, rethinking the educational experience of Egypt, what we have said elsewhere may be a fitting conclusion to this book:

> Democracy is a messy system, but it has survived because there is a sphere for debates and a set of rules that people follow even if they

don't benefit from them. Schools and universities for democratic communities cannot be less committed to expanding the democratic discourse and to challenging the political economy of capitalism. Without a serious exploration of the intersections between cultural diversity, affirmative action, and citizenship, the plural bases for democracy and the democratic discourse per se are at risk. Without a technically competent, ethically sound, spiritually engaging, and political feasible theory and practice of democratic multicultural citizenship, the people will perish. (Torres 1998, 259)

Particularly in the Middle East the people *will* perish. This is not a rhetorical device to speak about spiritual consciousness of the people, but to their own existential experience. The people will perish if the United States continues to export democracy through war and violence (Chomsky 2003), if authoritarian governments continue to preserve elite privilege without creating models of social distribution that are transparent and socially just, and if the great divider of Middle East policies, the tragic interaction between the Palestinian people and the State of Israel, is not resolved, once and for all, with a rational and practical way to achieve lasting social justice and peace.

Education cannot really change society, and cannot be exempted from the contradictions of social life and policy, as is clear through the lessons of this book. Yet we find ourselves in a terrible dilemma. We may abandon the struggle for freedom in our schools, falling pray to a nihilist perspective, or leave the schools and educational systems drifting in their own contradictions trying to promote social and cultural change from outside educational institutions. If the option is nihilism inside the educational system, or abandoning the systems pursuing change in the outside, we have lost the democratic dream. These choices, from an ethical grounded perspective as Freire invited us in the epigraph, are totally unacceptable.

Freire's contribution to understanding education as the act of freedom is an invitation to see the interminable dialectics in the struggle to free ourselves and to free others from constraints to freedom. Certainly, education as the act of freedom implies a different perspective on local, socially constructed, and generationally transmitted knowledge. It also implies a perspective that challenges normal science and nonparticipatory planning, and implies the construction of a theoretical and methodological perspective that is always suspicious of any scientific relationship that conceals relationships of domination. At the same time, while freedom is still to be conquered, freedom can be conquered because unequal, exploitative relationships are built by human beings and can be changed by human beings.

Critique and utopia, in the best of the Critical Theory tradition, has informed the workings of this book. While many of its conclusions could sound depressing, one may simply listen to the past, to the history, to the people who have overcome centuries of oppressive behaviors and government, and say with the Chicana and Chicano movements in the United States, "*si se puede.*" Moreover, if one wants to tap into the essence of the revolutionary movements thinking of education for social transformation, one could simply say in the spirit of Ernesto "Che" Guevara, "*la lucha continua.*"

Notes to Conclusion

1. This is the essence of the argument we put forward with Adriana Puiggrós trying to explain the loss of the tradition of normalism in Latin America, the growing gap between schooling and children and youth cultures and the growing uneasiness of teachers trying to do their work when schooling is being charged with more and more responsibilities in addressing the crisis of legitimacy of capitalist societies (Torres and Puiggrós 1996).

2. The recent reauthorization of the International Education Act through the efforts of a group of conservative academics and legislators gave rise to a most threatening development in US academia. The Act requires that universities receiving federal funding in education form a watchdog committee to monitor their research and teaching activities of the universities. Needless to say, this proposal has been met with a barrage of criticism, with many people equating the committee and its task with the infamous McCarthy hearings. For a contemporary treatment of the assaults on academic freedom in universities in the United States post- September 11 2001, see Beshara Doumani (2006).

References

Amnesty International. 2004. *Commission on Human Rights, 60th Session (15 March–23 April 2004) The human rights scandal of Guantanamo Bay–Amnesty International.* (http://www.amnesty.org/results/is/eng) (http://web.amnesty.org/pages/guantanamobay-index-eng)

Apple, Michael. 2003. *The State and Politics of Knowledge.* Falmer Press. Barrios de Pie book.

Benjamin, Walter. 1968. *Illuminations.* New York: Schocken Books.

Bourdieu, Pierre, and Jean Claude Passeron. 1990. *Reproduction in education, society, and culture.* London: Sage.

Bowles, Samuel, and Herbert Gintis. 1986. *Schooling in capitalist America: Educational reform and the contradictions of economic life.* New York: Basic Books.

Burbules, Nicholas C., and Carlos A.Torres. 2000. *Education and globalization: Critical perspectives.* New York: Routledge.

Chomsky, Noam. 2003. *Middle East illusions: Including peace in the Middle East: Reflections on justice and nationhood.* Chicago: Rowman and Littlefield.

Doumani, Beshara. 2006. *Academic freedom after September 11.* New York: Zone Books.

Freire, Paulo.1998b. *Politics and education.* Los Angeles: UCLA Latin American Center Publications.

———. 1998. *Pedagogy of freedom; Ethics, democracy, and civic courage.* Boston: Rowman and Littlefield.

Gadotti, Moacir. 2004. *Mestres do Rosseau.* São Paulo: Cortez Editores.

Kellner, Douglas. 1989. *Critical Theory, Marxism and Modernity.* Baltimore: The Johns Hopkins University Press.

Morrow, Raymond, and Carlos A. Torres. 2002. *Reading Freire and Habermas: Critical pedagogy and transformative social change.* New York: Teachers College Press.

Morrow, Raymond Allen, and David D. Brown. 1994. *Critical theory and methodology.* Thousand Oaks, London and New Delhi: Sage Publications. *Perdida al Atardecer.* Valencia: Germania.

Sahgal, Gita, and Nira Yuval-Davis. 2003. The Uses of Fundamentalism. In *Feminist Postcolonial Theory,* ed. Reina Lewis and Sara Mills, 43–48. New York: Routledge.

Samoff, Joel, and Bidemi Carrol. 2003. From Manpower Planning to the Knowledge Era: World Bank Policies on Higher Education in Africa. *Prepared for the UNESCO Forum on Higher Education, Research and Knowledge,* 15 July.

Torres, Carlos Alberto, and Adriana Puiggros, eds. 1996. *Education in Latin America: Comparative perspectives.* Boulder, CO: Westview Press.

Torres, Carlos Alberto. 1978. *Entrevistas con Paulo Freire.* Mexico: Gernika.

———. 1992. *The church, society and hegemony. A critical sociology of religion in Latin America.* Westport, CT and London: Praeger.

———. 1994. Intellectuals and University Life: Paulo Freire on Higher Education. Introduction. In *Paulo Freire at the National University in Mexico. A Dialogue,* ed. Gilberto Guevara Niebla, Alfredo L. Fernandez and Miguel Escobar, 1–25. Albany: State University of New York Press.

———. 1998. *Democracy, education, and multiculturalism: Dilemmas of citizenship in a global world.* Lanham, MD: Rowman and Littlefield.

———. 2004. The No Child Left Behind Act and American Politics. *Social Policy, a Journal of Socialist Thought.*

———. 2004. Requiem por Paulo Reglus Neves Freire. In *Poesía*

———. 2005. Expert Knowledge, External Assistance and Educational Reform in the Age of Neoliberalism: A Focus on the World Bank and Question of Moral Responsibilities in Third World Educational Reform. UCLA mimeographed.

Wallerstein, Emmanuel. 2004. *World-systems analysis: An introduction.* Durham, NC: Duke University Press.

Weiner, Lois. 1998. Schooling to Work. In *Post-Work. The Wages of Cybernation,* ed. Stanley Aronowitz and J. Cutler, 185–201. New York: Routledge.

Contributors

Iman Farag is Researcher in Political Sociology at the Centre d'Études et de Documentation Écononmique, Juridique et Sociale (CEDEJ), Cairo. She obtained her PhD, entitled *The Social Construction of National Education; Egypt 1900-1950,* in Political Sociology at the École des Hautes Etudes, Paris, in 1999. Her main fields of interest are the construction of public debates, the forms of political mobilizations, and the historical sociology of the political and social dimensions of education.

Linda Herrera is Senior Lecturer (Associate Professor) in Development Studies, with a focus on youth, at the Institute of Social Studies, The Hague. She obtained her PhD from Columbia University (2000) in comparative international education, with a concentration in Anthropology. During her residence in Egypt (1986-2003) she worked extensively in educational research and social science capacity-building. Her current research interests are youth cultures and the politics of development, and education in Muslim societies.

Fadia Maugith is an independent researcher and poet. She obtained her PhD in the department of the Philosophy of Education, Tanta University, Egypt, in 2003. Her dissertation addresses the political participation of university students. A long-time political activist, she is especially committed to women's equity and social justice.

Kamal Naguib is Professor in the Department of Curriculum and Methods of Teaching of the Faculty of Education, Alexandria University. He obtained his PhD in Education at the University of Pittsburgh in

1982. He was a founding member of the Society of the Sociology of Education of the League of Modern Education in Egypt (1982), the first group to apply concepts of critical pedagogy to the Egyptian context. He contributes regularly to media debates on education and critical democracy. His scholarly works address a range of subjects from the philosophy and critical theory of education, education and neoliberalism, to the sociology of teaching, and the political thought of students and teachers.

Ahmed Youssof Saad is Professor at the National Centre for Educational Research and Development, Cairo. He obtained his PhD at Ain Shams University and wrote his dissertation on education and public opinion in Egypt. He is a frequent contributor to the Arabic press. In addition to his many academic writings in Arabic on critical theory in education, civic education, human rights, and critical pedagogy, he has a keen interest in fiction writing and has authored a number of children's stories and short stories.

Carlos Alberto Torres is Professor of Social Sciences and Comparative Education in the Graduate School of Education, University of California, Los Angeles (UCLA) and Director, Paulo Freire Institute at UCLA. He is also the Founding Director of the Paulo Freire Institute in São Paulo, Brazil. He has authored over forty books and one hundred forty articles in Spanish, English, and Portuguese, ranging from the sociology of education, globalization, multiculturalism, critical social theory, and religion, not to mention his more recent works of poetry and short stories. He is an authority on Latin American education, and principal biographer of Brazilian philosopher and critical social theorist, Paulo Freire.

Index